A Linguistics Workbook

A Linguistics Workbook

Ann K. Farmer
Richard A. Demers

Third Edition

The MIT Press
Cambridge, Massachusetts
London, England

This book was set in Univers and
Times Roman by Asco Trade
Typesetting Ltd., Hong Kong and was
printed and bound in the United
States of America.

Excerpt from *A Clockwork Orange* by
Anthony Burgess reprinted by
permission of W. W. Norton &
Company, Inc. and William
Heinemann Ltd. Copyright © 1963 by
W. W. Norton & Company, Inc.
Copyright © 1962 by Anthony
Burgess.

Part II, Chamber Music, phonetically
transcribed, from *Collected Poems* by
James Joyce. Copyright 1918 by B. S.
Huebsch, Inc. Copyright 1927, 1936
by James Joyce. Copyright 1946 by
James Joyce. Reprinted by permission
of Viking Penguin Inc.

ISBN 0-262-56091-7

Contents

4 Syntax

5 Semantics

6 Language Variation

7 Language Change

8 Pragmatics

9 Psychology of Language

Appendixes

Bibliography

Preface

Our goal in preparing the third edition of this workbook has remained essentially the same as in preparing the first and second: to offer students experience with a broader range of languages than is provided in *Linguistics: An Introduction to Language and Communication*. *Linguistics* focuses for the most part on the properties of English. As stated there, the main reason for this is that "it is essential that students be able to evaluate critically our factual claims at each step, for this encourages a healthy skepticism and an active approach toward the subject matter" (p. xii). Given that students have at least some command of English, we can assume that they are able to draw upon this knowledge to formulate, test, and revise linguistic hypotheses. Thus, they are introduced to the basic methodology of linguistics as a science.

Nevertheless, it is extremely important that students become familiar with the structural properties of languages other than English. In *A Linguistics Workbook*, therefore, we have provided exercises based on a wide variety of the world's languages. We have preserved most of the exercises from the second edition, though we have dropped some and have added 10 new ones. (Two of the new exercises involve investigating problems that traditional grammars encounter when trying to legislate the "proper" use of pronouns.) In general, we continue to work toward improving the clarity of the exercises and broadening the scope of the workbook in terms of languages covered. In several chapters we have selected material from particular languages because they illustrate a desired range of structural types. We invite students to look for similarities and common themes amid the structural diversity. In this way they begin to carry out one of the central goals of current linguistic theory: to discover the basic and shared organizing principles of human language.

As in the second edition, the chapters follow the order of presentation in *Linguistics*; thus, the chapter on morphology precedes the chapters on phonetics, phonology, and syntax. We prefer this order for two reasons. First, students have little difficulty relating to words, as opposed to perhaps less intuitively obvious units such as distinctive features. Second, words encode not only morphological information but also phonological, syntactic, semantic, and pragmatic information; thus, the word can serve as an intelligible and unintimidating introduction to some of the basic concepts of linguistics.

This edition of the workbook also follows the first two in that several of the exercises in the chapter on pragmatics would traditionally be placed in a syntax section. Even though these exercises require the student to recognize certain syntactic properties and regularities, we have placed them in the chapter on pragmatics in order to illustrate the numerous ways in which the major moods can be marked in the world's languages. In our exercises on moods we have also included examples of sentence negation, since negation frequently patterns with mood marking.

We have removed numerous "word building" exercises from the morphology chapter and placed them in the syntax chapter, designating them as "morphosyntax" problems.

The exercises in this workbook vary in difficulty. This range makes the workbook appropriate for use in intermediate linguistics courses as well as introductory ones. The more difficult exercises also serve another purpose. There are frequently students who become extremely interested in linguistics and wish to do extra work. We have found that many of these exercises are both challenging and stimulating for such students.

We should also call attention to the following point. When one is dealing with a large number of languages, the problem of consistency across writing systems becomes very complex. For example, the symbol *a* (print-*a*) is typically used in texts to represent a lax low back vowel. In phonetic writing systems, however, the symbol for a lax low back vowel is *a* (script-*a*). We have nevertheless represented almost all of the low back vowels as *a*, in conformity with standard (not phonetic) convention. Unless otherwise noted, the user of this workbook should assume that the symbol *a* represents a lax low back vowel.

Finally, linguists are fond of saying that the best way to learn about linguistics is to *do* linguistics. This workbook is intended to make doing linguistics possible at an introductory level. We hope that students will find the exercises both interesting and instructive.

Acknowledgments

Many people have been involved in the preparation of this workbook. First, we would like to thank those who contributed the basic ideas for our preliminary versions of exercises: Jonathan Beck (French, 3.8, 3.9), Lee Bickmore (Korean, 3.2), Kathy Budway (Spanish, 2.5), Ken Hale, who helped us with the Dyirbal (4.15) and Navajo (8.14) problems, Barbara Hollenbach (Copala Trique, 8.12), and Adrienne Lehrer, who suggested the idea behind the Indo-European exercises (7.1, 7.2).

We would also like to thank the following people who checked particular exercises and data for us: Julia Annas (British English, 6.3), Adele Barker (Russian, 1.5, 4.24), Jim Cathey (Finnish, 8.11), Christiane Dechert (German, 4.11), Hiroko Ikawa (Japanese, 4.25), Rich Janda (assisted by Sue Foster), who first used the original version of the British dialect story (6.3) as an exercise at the University of Arizona, Eloise Jelinek (Yaqui, 4.14), Margaret Jeun (Korean, 3.2), Soowon Kim (Korean, 3.2), Steve Lapointe and his students (Japanese, 4.25), Stan Lekach (Russian, 1.5, 4.24), Bruce Peng (Mandarin Chinese, 8.13), Sirpa Saletta (Finnish, 8.11), Kyung-Hee Seo (Korean, 3.2), Amy Sung (Korean 3.2), Natsuko Tsujimura (all the Japanese exercises), Virginia Valian (1.6), Mary Willie (Navajo, 8.14), Moira Yip, and Ofelia Zepeda (Tohono O'odham, 1.8, 1.9, 3.3, 4.13).

Ken Hale and Donna Jo Napoli deserve special thanks for reading an earlier version of this workbook in its entirety and making valuable suggestions.

We would like to thank Mark Farmer for the drawings that appear throughout the workbook and Charlie H. Adams for allowing us to use two of her poems in exercise 2.3.

We are grateful, once again, to Anne Mark for her continued role as copy editor. We always rely on her skill and informed feedback to bring this project to successful completion.

Finally, we thank the many students who worked on various versions of these exercises. We have continued to improve the exercises, and to add new ones (and even delete some), based on our students' invaluable input. We would like to think that they learned positive things about linguistics in spite of the fact that the preliminary drafts of virtually all of the exercises needed subsequent refining.

1 Morphology

1.1 A Clockwork Orange: *Meaning and Form in Context*

The passage below is taken from Anthony Burgess's novel *A Clockwork Orange.* Many of the vocabulary items are borrowed (loosely) from Russian. First read the passage, trying to match the "new" words (underlined) with the definitions given in question A. Both structural (syntactic and morphological) clues and context will be helpful in figuring out what the words mean. Then answer questions A and B.

There was me, that is Alex, and my three droogs, that is Pete, Georgie, and Dim, Dim being really dim, and we sat in the Korova Milkbar making up our rassoodocks what to do with the evening, ... The Korova Milkbar was a milkplus mesto, and you may, O my brothers, have forgotten what these mestos were like, things changing so skorry these days and everybody very quick to forget, newspapers not being read much neither. Well, what they sold there was milk plus something else. They had no licence for selling liquor, but there was no law yet against prodding some of the new veshches which they used to put into the old moloko, so you could peet it with vellocet or synthemesc or drencrom or one or two other veshches which would give you a nice quiet horrorshow fifteen minutes admiring Bog And All His Holy Angels And Saints in your left shoe with lights bursting all over your mozg. Or you could peet milk with knives in it, as we used to say, and this would sharpen you up ... and that was what we were peeting this evening I'm starting off the story with.

Questions

A. Match each underlined word in the text with one of the definitions on the right, as shown in the first example. (Note: N = noun, V = verb, Adv = adverb)

	Word	Definition
1.	droog	friend (N)
2.	Bog	God (N)
3.	vellocat	a drug* (N)
	synthemesc	
	drencrom	

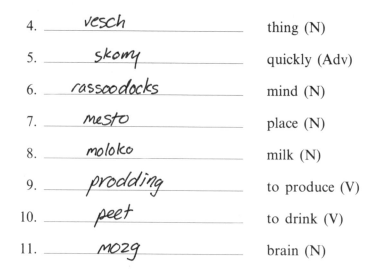

4. _____vesch_____   thing (N)

5. _____skomy_____   quickly (Adv)

6. ____rassoodocks____   mind (N)

7. _____mesto_____   place (N)

8. _____moloko_____   milk (N)

9. _____prodding_____   to produce (V)

10. _____peet_____   to drink (V)

11. _____mozg_____   brain (N)

*These three words are probably *not* borrowed from Russian.

B. Provide morphological evidence (and syntactic evidence as well, if you can) to support your choices in question A. The first space is filled in as an example.

  1. *droog*. Evidence that *droog* is a noun: (Morphological) The plural -*s* is attached to *droog*. (Syntactic) *Droog* occurs in the phrase *my three droogs*. Nouns combine with possessive pronouns (*my*, *his*) and adjectives (*three*, *red*, *happy*) to form noun phrases.

     Context suggests that *droog* refers to Alex's companions. The definition most compatible with *droog*, then, is "friend."

  2.

  3.

4.

5.

6.

7.

8.

9.

10.

11.

6

Name *Jeremy Garber*

Section

1.2 Open- and Closed-Class Words

Read the following passage. For each underlined word, answer questions A–E. (A review of pages 18–23 and 36–39 of *Linguistics* will be helpful.) The answers to the questions for the word *meaning* are given as an example.

... almost self-evidently, a style is specific: its meaning is part and parcel of its period, and cannot be transposed innocently. To see other *periods* as mirrors of our own is to turn history into narcissism; to see other *styles* as open to our own style is to turn history into a dream. But such, really, is the dream of the pluralist: he seems to sleepwalk in the museum. (Foster 1982)

Questions

A. Is the word an *open-class* or *closed-class* word?

B. Is the word *simple* or *complex*?

C. For each complex word, identify its pieces. That is, does it have a prefix or a suffix? If it has a suffix, is the suffix inflectional or derivational?

D. What category (part of speech) does the word belong to?

E. What morphological evidence can you provide to support your answer to question D?

1. *meaning*. (A) open-class word; (B) complex; (C) *mean + ing* (stem + suffix), *-ing* is derivational; (D) *meaning* is a noun; (E) *-ing* attaches to verbs to create nouns. Note that an *-ing* morpheme does attach to verbs to create verbs (e.g., *walk + ing* as in *John was walking the dog*). We know, however, that the *-ing* in *meaning* is a noun-forming suffix rather than a verb-forming suffix because the plural morpheme *-s* can be attached to it: *its meanings are part and parcel of its period*. The plural morpheme cannot be attached to *walking*: **John was walkings the dog*.

2. self-evidently

A. open-class
B. complex
D. adverb
E. It ends in -ly.

3. its

A. closed-class
B. complex
D. possessive pronoun
E. there is none

4. transposed

A. open-class
B. complex
D. verb
E. it has the "-ed" of a conjugated verb

5. narcissism

A. open-class
B. complex
D. noun
E. it can be changed into "narcissisms"

"-ism" is also an understood noun marker.

6. into

A. closed-class
B. complex
D. preposition
E. There is none

7. sleepwalk

A. open-class
B. complex
D. verb
E. It can be conjugated into "sleepwalks" or "sleepwalking."

8. the

A. closed-class
B. simple
D. article
E. There is none.

Name _____

Section _____

1.3 Compound and Noun Phrase Ambiguities

English words can combine to form compound words, sometimes referred to simply as *compounds* (such as *car-phone, windmill, golf club*). A major indicator that a sequence of two words is a compound is that the relative prominence (emphasis, stress) occurs on the first word. Consider the words *green* and *house*. The sequence *green house* is a compound if *green* is emphasized (represented here as *GREEN house*). A *GREEN house* is a building, usually made of glass, in which plants are grown. However, if the word *house* is stressed (*green HOUSE*), then the sequence *green house* is not a compound but a noun phrase that is composed of the adjective *green* modifying the noun *house*. Thus, a *green HOUSE* is a house that is green.

There are other differences between noun phrases and compounds. First, the comparative *-er*, which attaches to adjectives (*richer, smaller*, etc.), can attach to *green* in the noun phrase *green HOUSE* to yield *greener house*. The compound interpretation is not possible in this case. Second, in the case of the noun phrase *green HOUSE* additional adjectives may be conjoined with *green*. For example, someone who talks about a *green and yellow house* is still referring to a house that is (in part) green. However, the expression *and yellow* cannot interrupt the members of a compound (**GREENandyellowhouse*).

Like simple nouns, compounds can be ambiguous. In fact, a compound can acquire a second or third meaning through the creative use of language. For example, *egg roll* can be used to refer either to a certain kind of Chinese food or to an activity that takes place (e.g., at the White House) around Easter.

For each pair of drawings, you are to determine (1) whether the combination of words under the drawing is an ambiguous compound (a compound that is associated with two different meanings, like the example *egg roll*) or (2) whether the combination of words can be understood *either* as a compound *or* as a noun phrase (like the example *green HOUSE/GREEN house*). Study the drawings and answer questions A, B, and (optionally) C.

1. Big-Wig

2. Fish-Tank

3. Big-Top

4. Cat-Food

5. White-Fish

6. Church-Key

7. Mouse-Trap

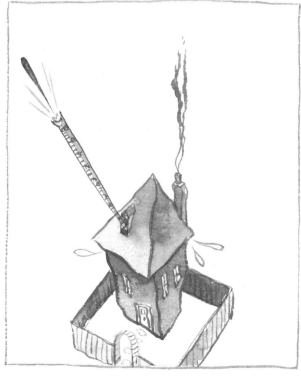

8. Hot-House

A. Which combinations of two words are ambiguous compound nouns? (List them by number.)

B. Which combinations of two words could be either a noun phrase or a compound noun? (List them by number.)

C. (*Optional*) Either draw or describe a drawing or situation similar to the pairs found in this exercise. That is, find a case of (1) a compound that has two possible meanings or (2) a case of a sequence of words that are interpretable either as a compound or as a noun phrase.

1.4 Word Building 1: -ness Affixation (English)

For this exercise, consider the following words:

List I	List II
1. furious	furiousness
2. infectious	infectiousness
3. courteous	courteousness
4. powerless	powerlessness
5. fair	fairness
6. clever	cleverness
7. warm	warmness
8. useful	usefulness
9. prideful	pridefulness
10. heavy	heaviness
11. slack	slackness
12. sick	sickness
13. sleepy	sleepiness

Questions

State the word formation rule for the affix -*ness*, using the following format (see *Linguistics*, pp. 28–34):

A. Phonological change

B. Category change
  1. What part of speech does -*ness* attach to? That is, what is the part of speech of the words in list I?

2. What is the part of speech of the derived word? That is, what is the part of speech of the words in list II?

C. Semantic change
   What meaning change is caused by the suffix -*ness*? That is, in the ideal case, what element of meaning does it contribute?

1.5 Word Building 2: -ščik Affixation (Russian)

Below are two lists of Russian words. The words in list II are derived from those in list I. After studying the lists, answer questions A–D.

The two symbols *šč* stand for the one letter щ in written Russian. The apostrophe (') after consonants indicates that the preceding consonant is palatalized. This phonetic feature does not play a role in the answer to this exercise, however.

The *-o* suffix on *derevo* indicates that it is a neuter noun; the *-a* suffix on *gazeta* indicates that it is a feminine noun. Ignore these suffixes for the purposes of this exercise and assume that the suffix under study attaches to the stems *derev-* and *gazet-*.

List I		List II	
Russian word	English gloss	Russian word	English gloss
1. atom	"atom"	atomščik	"atomic-warmonger"
2. baraban	"drum"	barabanščik	"drummer"
3. kalambur	"pun"	kalamburščik	"punner"
4. pulemyot	"machine-gun"	pulemyotčik	"machine-gunner"
5. mebel'	"furniture"	mebel'ščik	"furniture maker"
6. beton	"concrete"	betonščik	"concrete worker"
7. lom	"scrap"	lomščik	"salvage collector"
8. derevo	"tree"	derevščik	"craftsman"
9. gazeta	"newspaper"	gazetčik	"newspaper seller" or "journalist"
10. lyot	"flight"	lyotčik	"flier" or "pilot"

Words 1–6 are from Townsend 1975, 174.

Questions

A. The suffix that attaches to the words in list I to form the words in list II has two forms. What are they?

-ščik and -čik

B. Given examples 1–10, suggest a possible reason why one form of the suffix occurs rather than the other. (Hint: Compare the ending of the stems of examples 4, 9, and 10 with the ending of the stems of all the other examples.)

when the stem ends in -t, the š is not pronounced

C. The suffix attaches to a noun to create a noun with a new meaning. How is the meaning of the derived word related to the meaning of the basic word in list I? (Obviously, unless you know Russian, you will have to base your hypothesis on the English glosses.)

The suffix means "one who utilizes X in a career."

D. Given the base *apparat-*, what would you predict to be the derived Russian word that results from the rule discussed above?

apparatčik

1.6 Word Building 3: -like Affixation (English)

Examine the data in lists I and II and answer questions A–F. It will be helpful to review the material in *Linguistics* on parts of speech (pp. 18–23).

	List I	List II
1.	war	warlike
2.	wife	wifelike
3.	king	kinglike
4.	prince	princelike
5.	human	humanlike
6.	snake	snakelike
7.	child	childlike
8.	lady	ladylike
9.	tree	treelike
10.	death	deathlike
11.	thumb	thumblike
12.	book	booklike
13.	sportsman	sportsmanlike
14.	dungeon	dungeonlike
15.	fish	fishlike

Questions

A. The morpheme *like* combines with a word of what category (part of speech)? That is, what category is *X* in *X-like*?

B. The words in list II all belong to what category?

C. What meaning change appears to be caused by *like*? That is, in the ideal case, what element of meaning does it contribute?

D. Have any of the examples in list II *drifted* in meaning? (See *Linguistics*, p. 42.) If so, which ones? In each case, how does the drifted meaning differ from the compositional meaning (i.e., the sum of the meaning of the stem, *X*, plus the meaning of *like*)?

E. Consider the following examples and answer the questions below:

idealike
justicelike
happinesslike

Can *like* combine with *any* word belonging to the category in your answer to question A? That is, can *any* word belonging to the same category as the words in list I combine with *like*? If there are restrictions, what do they appear to be?

F. Does *like* combine *only* with words of the category exemplified in list I, or can it combine with words from other categories as well? Give examples and explain.

1.7 Word Building 4: Turkish

Study the Turkish expressions below and answer questions A–C.

	Turkish form	English gloss
1.	el	"the hand"
2.	eller	"hands"
3.	elim	"my hand"
4.	ev	"the house"
5.	eve	"to the house"
6.	ellerimiz	"our hands"
7.	ellerimde	"in my hands"
8.	evlerde	"in the houses"
9.	evden	"from the house"
10.	ellerim	"my hands"
11.	ellerinize	"to your (pl.) hands"
12.	evlerim	"my houses"
13.	elin	"your (sg.) hand"
14.	evimiz	"our house"
15.	evde	"in the house"
16.	elimde	"in my hand"
17.	evlerimiz	"our houses"
18.	evlerimden	"from my houses"
19.	evleriniz	"your (pl.) houses"
20.	evim	"my house"
21.	ellerimden	"from my hands"
22.	evler	"houses"
23.	eline	"to your (sg.) hand"
24.	ellerin	"your (sg.) hands"
25.	elimden	"from my hand"
26.	evine	"to your (sg.) house"

In the English translations, *your* is listed as singular (*sg.*) when it refers to one person and as plural (*pl.*) when it refers to more than one person.

Questions

A. In the spaces below, list the Turkish morphemes that correspond to the English words on the right.

Turkish morpheme   English gloss

1. _el_   "(the) hand"

2. _ev_   "(the) house"

3. _-ler_   plural

4. _-im_   "my"

5. _-imiz_   "our"

6. _-in_   "your (sg.)"

7. _-iniz_   "your (pl.)"

8. _-e_   "to"

9. _-de_   "in"

10. _-den_   "from"

B. Given the Turkish data, what is the order of the morphemes (indicating possession, person, etc.) of the suffixes in a word?

noun, pluralization, possession, preposition

C. Based on your answers in questions A and B, how would you translate the following English forms into Turkish?

1. from your house   _evinden_

2. to our house   _evimize_

3. in my house   _evimde_

Name *Jeremy Gawber*

Section

1.8 Word Building 5: Tohono O'odham

Consider the following data from Tohono O'odham, a Native American language belonging to the Uto-Aztecan family, and answer questions A–C.

The symbol ' stands for a consonant known as a glottal stop. (A glottal stop is found at the beginning of the two *oh*'s in the English expression *oh-oh*. The glottal stop between the two *oh*'s is the easier to hear and even feel.) The symbol *:* indicates that the vowel preceding it is long (hence, *o:* is a long *o*). The symbol *ñ* is pronounced like the Spanish *ñ* or the English sequence *ny* in *canyon*. The symbol ˘ indicates that a vowel is short (hence, *ĭ* is short). A dot under a consonant indicates a special pronunciation with the tongue slightly curled back. The orthographic symbols are those now employed by the Tohono O'odham people. For a discussion of the phonetic value of the orthographic symbol *e*, see exercise 3.3.

	List I		List II	
	Tohono O'odham form	English gloss	Tohono O'odham form	English gloss
1.	je'e	"mother"	ñje'e	"my mother"
2.	'o:gĭ	"father"	m'o:gĭ	"your father"
3.	kakkio	"legs"	hakakkio	"their legs"
4.	no:nowĭ	"hands"	'emno:nowĭ	"your (pl.) hands"
5.	'o'ohana	"books"	t'o'ohana	"our books"
6.	kotoñ	"shirt"	kotoñij	"his/her shirt"
7.	wopnam	"hats"	twopnam	"our hats"
8.	mamgina	"cars"	'emmamgina	"your (pl.) cars"
9.	papla	"shovels"	hapapla	"their shovels"
10.	hoa	"basket"	ñhoa	"my basket"
11.	taḍ	"foot"	taḍij	"his/her foot"
12.	ki:	"house"	mki:	"your house"
13.	na:nk	"ears"	'emna:nk	"your (pl.) ears"
14.	to:ton	"knees"	hato:ton	"their knees"
15.	we:nag	"sibling"	we:nagij	"his/her sibling"
16.	si:l	"saddle"	ñsi:l	"my saddle"
17.	taḍ	"foot"	mtaḍ	"your foot"
18.	mo:mĭ	"heads"	tmo:mĭ	"our heads"
19.	na:nk	"ears"	na:nkij	"his/her ears"
20.	kakkio	"legs"	'emkakkio	"your (pl.) legs"
21.	wuhi	"eye"	ñwuhi	"my eye"
22.	mamgina	"cars"	tmamgina	"our cars"
23.	da:k	"nose"	ñda:k	"my nose"
24.	da:k	"nose"	da:kij	"his/her nose"

A. For each of the following possessive words of English, list the corresponding possessive morpheme in Tohono O'odham.

1. Possessive morpheme

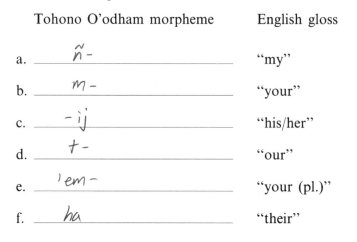

	Tohono O'odham morpheme	English gloss
a.	ñ̃ -	"my"
b.	m -	"your"
c.	-ij'	"his/her"
d.	t -	"our"
e.	'em -	"your (pl.)"
f.	ha	"their"

B. The Tohono O'odham possessive morphemes are bound morphemes. Are they prefixes or suffixes?

prefixes

C. What is special about the third person singular possessive morpheme (meaning "his/her") in Tohono O'odham?

it is a suffix rather than a prefix

Section

1.9 Word Building 6: Tohono O'odham

Consider the following verb forms from Tohono O'odham and answer questions A and B. (The special symbols used in writing these Tohono O'odham forms are explained in exercise 1.8.)

Tohono O'odham form	English gloss
Singular	
1. ñeok	"speaks"
2. him	"walks"
3. dagkon	"wipes"
4. helwuin	"is sliding"
5. 'ul	"sticks out"
Plural	
1. ñeñeok	"we/you/they speak"
2. hihim	"we/you/they walk"
3. dadagkon	"we/you/they wipe"
4. hehelwuin	"we/you/they are sliding"
5. 'u'ul	"we/you/they stick out"

Questions

A. Describe, as precisely as you can, how the plural verbs are formed from the singular verbs. (What must be done to a singular form in order to convert it into a plural form?)

First consonant + first vowel are repeated at the beginning of the word.

B. What is the name of the morphological process illustrated in the data? (Review the discussion of affixes in *Linguistics*, pp. 18–21).

reduplication

2 Phonetics

C. The *f*-sound is associated with a number of different orthographic (letter) representations. Provide at least 3 different examples.

enou*gh*

*f*un

*ph*ilistine

D. The letters *b* and *p* do not stand for any sound in the following examples:

b: climb, dumber, crumb
p: psychology, pneumonia, pneumatic

Find 5 additional words containing letters that apparently do not stand for any sound. Underline the letter that is not pronounced.

*m*nemonics   gna*t*

tong*u*e   *k*night

sie*v*e

a*c*knowle*d*ge

*k*nack

2.2 English Orthography 2: Plural

The English plural suffix -*s*, discussed in chapter 3 of *Linguistics*, has different pronunciations. Study the data provided in the list below, and answer the question that follows.

Singular noun	Plural noun	Pronunciation of -*s*
bough	boughs	*z*-sound
cough	coughs	*s*-sound
bride	brides	*z*-sound
pâté	pâtés	*z*-sound
attribute	attributes	*s*-sound
avenue	avenues	*z*-sound
Basque	Basques	*s*-sound
beret	berets	*z*-sound
pot	pots	*s*-sound

Question

Is it possible to predict the pronunciation of the plural morpheme from the way the noun to which it is attached is *spelled*? Explain why or why not. Base your answer on the data above.

2.3 Reverse Transcription

Question

Below are the phonetic transcriptions of three poems. The first is an untitled poem by James Joyce (1946). The second and third are "Benediction for Henry Frog" and "Mud Song" by Charlie H. Adams. In the spaces provided between lines, write a reverse transcription of any 2 of these poems (that is, give their original orthographic representation).

Poem 1

1. ðʌ twaylayt tṛnz frʌm æməθɪst
   The twilight turns from amethyst

2. tuw diyp ænd diypṛ bluw.
   to deep and deeper blue.

3. ðʌ læmp fɪlz wɪθ ʌ peyl griyn glow
   The lamp fills with a pale green glow

4. ðʌ triyz ʌv ðʌ ævənuw.
   The trees of the avenue.

5. ðʌ owld piyænow pleyz æn ɛr,
   The old piano plays an air,

6. sədeyt ænd slow ænd gey.
   Sedate and slow and gay.

7. šiy bɛnz əpan ðʌ yɛlow kiyz,
   She bends upon the yellow keys

8. hṛ hɛd ɪnklaynz ðɪs wey.
   Her head inclines this ways.

9. šay θats* ænd greyv wayd ayz ænd hænz
   Shy thoughts and grave wide eyes and hands

10. ðæt wandṛ æz ðey lɪst—
    that wander as they list

11. ðʌ twaylayt tṛnz tuw darkṛ bluw

The ~~tw~~ twilight turns to darker blue

12. wıθ layts ʌv æməθıst.

with lights of amethyst.

*(or θɔts, depending on the dialect)

Poem 2

1. hır layz ɑr frɛnd, hɛnriy frɔg.

2. hiy dıd nɔt lænd, wɛn hiy lɛpt, ın ðʌ bɔg.

3. hız mʌðṛz wayz kawnsɛl hiy dıd nɔt kiyp:

4. "yuw mʌst alweyz lʊk, biyfɔr yuw liyp."

5. bʌt hɛnriy dıdınt ænd lændid ınstɛd

6. ın ðʌ bʌtṛ, ænd ðɛn ın ðʌ flawṛbɛd…

7. ʌndṛ ðʌ flawṛz.

8. nɛkst taym rawnd, mey hɛnriy kʌm ʌp

9. ʌ lʌvliy, gowldṇ bʌtṛkʌp.

Poem 3

1. mʌd, ow ðʌ uwš, ow ðʌ muwš, ow ðʌ smuwš ʌf it.

Mud, o the oosh, o the moosh, o the smoosh of it.

2. slıpıŋ ænd slaydıŋ, ænd slɔgıŋ ʌlɔŋ.

Slipping and sliding, and slogging along.

3. ıt uwzız. ıt slṛps, ænd ıt bṛps, ænd ıt bʌmbḷz.

It oozes. It slurps, and it burps, and it bumbles.

4. ıt slʌmps, ænd ıt bʌmps, ænd ıt lʌmps, ænd ıt jʌmbḷz.

It slumps and it bumps, and it lumps, and it jumbles.

5. mʌd hæz now ɛjız. ıt jʌst rowlz ænd mʌdḷz.

36

6. ðʌ mɔr yuw dəfayn ɪt, ðʌ mɔr ɪt bʌfʌd̩z.

7. ɪz ɪt pʊdɪŋ? spəgɛtiy? ɔr tæfiy? ɔr ǰɛlow?

8. ɔr θɪk meypḷ sɹəp? ɔr čaklɛt maršmɛlow?

9. wɪθ ðʌ klæmz, sneyḷz ænd wɹmz, wiy ɑr gɛsɪŋ guwp.

10. bʌt ðʌ dʌks now ðʌ ænsɹ̩. wɪr ɪn ðʌ dʌk suwp.

2.4 Transcription: Monosyllables

Question

Write the following monosyllabic words using the transcription system given in appendix 3. Be sure not to be fooled by the orthography.

1. fish	fɪš	16. plan	plæn	31. laugh	læf
2. thin	θɪn	17. pooch	puwč	32. rough	rʌf
3. then	ðɛn	18. pouch	pawč	33. thought	θɔt
4. hitch	hɪč	19. peach	pìyč	34. drought	drawt
5. ping	pɪŋ	20. rouge	ruwž	35. though	ðow
6. taste	teyst	21. dew	diyuw	36. cog	kag
7. sheep	šiyp	22. do	duw	37. clinch	klɪnč
8. try	tray	23. due	dyuw	38. raw	rɔ
9. live	lɪv	24. fin	fɪn	39. lawn	lɔn
10. life	layf	25. vine	vayn	40. gone	gan
11. jut	ǰʌt	26. roof	ruf	41. lath	læθ
12. Goth	gɔθ	27. bang	bæŋ ·	42. lathe	leyð
13. juke	ǰuwk	28. dung	dʌŋ	43. soot	sut
14. hoof	huf	29. with	wɪθ	44. crush	krʌš
15. hooves	huwz	30. width	wɪdθ	45. ought	ɔt

Name _____

Section _____

2.5 Phonetic Variation: Spanish /b/, /d/, /g/

Below is a broad transcription of some Spanish words. [b]/[β], [d]/[ð], and [g]/[ɣ] are pairs of allophones whose members are in complementary distribution; that is, they occur in mutually exclusive (or nonoverlapping) phonetic environments. (See *Linguistics*, pp. 85–89.)

[β] is a voiced bilabial fricative.
[ð] is a voiced interdental fricative.
[ɣ] is a voiced dorsovelar fricative.

	Spanish form	English gloss		Spanish form	English gloss
1.	[aɣrio]	"sour"	14.	[kaβe]	"it fits"
2.	[gustar]	"to please"	15.	[eðað]	"age"
3.	[xweɣo]	"game"	16.	[komuniðað]	"community"
4.	[albondiɣas]	"meatballs"	17.	[deðo]	"finger/toe"
5.	[gastos]	"expenses"	18.	[droɣas]	"drugs"
6.	[gonsales]	surname	19.	[seða]	"silk"
7.	[ɣaɣa]	"sore, boil"	20.	[ganaðo]	"cattle"
8.	[uβa]	"grape"	21.	[usteð]	"you (sg. polite)"
9.	[futbol]	"soccer"	22.	[bastante]	"plenty"
10.	[kaldo]	"broth"	23.	[brinkar]	"to jump"
11.	[algo]	"something"	24.	[suβo]	"I climb"
12.	[sombra]	"shade"	25.	[uβo]	"there was"
13.	[saβino]	"cypress"	26.	[kluβ]	"club"

Questions

A. When do the voiced stops [b], [d], and [g] occur?

B. When do the voiced fricatives [β], [ð], and [ɣ] occur?

C. Given the distribution of the voiced stops versus the voiced fricatives described in your answers to questions A and B, decide which sounds ([b], [d], [g] *or* [β], [ð], [ɣ]) are basic and which are derived.

2.6 Word Building: -ity Suffixation

When an affix is attached to a stem (or word) to create a new word, a nontrivial phonological change may occur (see *Linguistics*, pp. 29–30). Lists I and II illustrate just such a case. Consider the two lists of words and the relation between them, and answer the questions that follow.

	List I	List II
1.	eccentric	eccentricity
2.	elastic	elasticity
3.	opaque	opacity
4.	electric	electricity
5.	peptic	pepticity
6.	specific	specificity
7.	periodic	periodicity
8.	endemic	endemicity
9.	volcanic	volcanicity
10.	centric	centricity
11.	egocentric	egocentricity

Questions

A. Transcribe the pairs of words in lists I and II in the spaces provided. Indicate the placement of main stress (e.g., *capable* /kéypəbļ/).

1. _____   _____

2. _____   _____

3. _____   _____

4. _____   _____

5. _____   _____

6. _____   _____

7. _____   _____

8. _____   _____

9. _____   _____

10. _____   _____

11. _____   _____

B. Describe what changes occur in the words in list I when the affix *-ity* is attached.

C. You may not be familiar with some of the words in the lists. However, you should have had no trouble determining where the main stress of the derived words (those in list II) is located. State a generalization about the position of the main stress in the words in list II.

2.7 Writing Systems: Japanese

The Japanese language can be written in several different ways. One method (*kanji*) is based on characters borrowed from the Chinese writing system. Another (*romaji*) uses letters from the roman alphabet; this system is used to write the Japanese in this workbook. Yet another writing system, the *katakana* syllabary, uses symbols that represent consonant-plus-vowel sequences (refer to *Linguistics*, pp. 537–542, for information on syllable-based writing systems). The chart below is a partial list of the symbols that make up the katakana syllabary of Japanese. Study the symbols and their pronunciations, and answer questions A–E.

1. カ /ka/　キ /ki/　ク /ku/　ケ /ke/　コ /ko/
2. サ /sa/　シ /ši/　ス /su/　セ /se/　ソ /so/
3. タ /ta/　チ /či/　ツ /tsu/　テ /te/　ト /to/
4. ナ /na/　ニ /ni/　ヌ /nu/　ネ /ne/　ノ /no/
5. ハ /ha/　ヒ /hi/　フ /fu/　ヘ /he/　ホ /ho/
6. マ /ma/　ミ /mi/　ム /mu/　メ /me/　モ /mo/

Questions

A. Consider the following examples:

1. ガ /ga/
2. ギ /gi/
3. グ /gu/
4. ゴ /go/

What important role does the diacritic ゛ play?

B. Based on your answer to question A, transcribe these symbols:

1. ザ /   /
2. デ /   /
3. ゼ /   /
4. ド /   /

C. Would it make sense for the diacritic ゛ to be added to any of the following symbols: ニ, ノ, マ, ム? Why or why not?

D. The diacritic ゛ indicates a voiced bilabial stop when associated with the symbols in line 5. Transcribe the following symbols. For example: バ /ba/.

1. ビ /   /
2. ブ /   /
3. ベ /   /
4. ボ /   /

E. The diacritic ° is combined with the katakana symbols in one of the above lines to indicate /pa/, /pi/, /pu/, /pe/, or /po/.

1. Write the katakana symbols that represent the following sound combinations. (The symbol ° should be written to the upper right of the basic symbols you have chosen.)

a. _____ /pa/

b. _____ /pi/

c. _____ /pu/

d. _____ /pe/

e. _____ /po/

2. Why did you choose the symbols you did?

3. What does the diacritic ° represent?

2.8 Special Topic 1: Transcription (Polysyllabics)

Questions

Write the following words using the transcription system given in appendix 3 and in *Linguistics* (pp. 66–67). Pay special attention to the reduced vowels (see *Linguistics*, pp. 75–76 and 119–125). There are two references to reduced vowels. The second reference explains the nature of reduced vowels: they are in the weak branch of the binary and ternary feet of English. Depending on your dialect, some of the words may have syllabic consonants.

Indicate the position of main stress by placing an accent mark over the stressed vowel. (Example: *maintain* /meyntéyn/) The syllable with the main stress will be the most prominent syllable. It will have a "stronger beat" or seem to be louder or more emphatic than the surrounding syllables. Note how related words may differ in the position of the main stress. The main stress is on the second (or final) syllable in *derive* but on the third syllable counting from the left in *derivátion*. Notice what happens to vowels that "lose" their stress.

A. 1. gymnast   /ǰímnəst/   6. explosion   /eksplóžən/

   2. gymnastics   /ǰImnǽstIks/   7. value   /vǽlyuw/

   3. present (verb) /priysɛ́nt/   8. evaluate   /iyvǽlyuweyt/

   4. present (noun) /prɛ́sənt/   9. deny   /diynáy/

   5. explode   /ɛksplówd/   10. denial   /dináyəl/

B. 1. either   /iyðə́r/   6. permit (verb) /pərmÍt/

   2. ether   /iyθə́r/   7. permit (noun) /pə́rmIt/

   3. torment (verb) /tɒwrmɛ́nt/   8. ardor   /árdər/

   4. torment (noun) /tówrmɛnt/   9. arduous   /árǰuwəs/

   5. torrent   /tɒwrɨnt/   10. saddle   /sǽdl̩/

C. 1. derive   /dəráyv/   6. example   /egzǽmpəl/

    2. derivation   /derɪváyšən/   7. exercise   /éksərsayz/

    3. apparent   /əpǽrɪnt/   8. erase   /iyréys/

    4. a parent   /ə pǽrɪnt/   9. erasure   /iyréyšər/

    5. accomplish   /əkámplɪš/   10. predatory   /prédɪtɔriy/

D. 1. congress   /cáŋgrɪs/   6. decide   /dəsáyd/

    2. congressional   /cəŋgréšənəl/   7. decision   /dəsɪ́žən/

    3. logic   /lájɪk/   8. decisive   /dəsáysɪv/

    4. logician   /ləjɪ́šən/   9. autocrat   /ɔ́təkræt/

    5. logicism   /lájɪsɪzm/   10. autocracy   /ɔtákrəsiy/

2.9 Special Topic 2: Transcription (Vowels before r)

Questions

Write the following words containing the phoneme /r/, using the transcription system given in appendix 3 and in *Linguistics* (review pp. 89–92).

A. 1. boor _____   6. dear _____

   2. bore _____   7. fir _____

   3. poor _____   8. mire _____

   4. care _____   9. sewer _____

   5. car _____   10. mirror _____

B. 1. tier _____   6. lawyer _____

   2. Bayer _____   7. earn _____

   3. merry _____   8. lower _____

   4. marry _____   9. sour _____

   5. Mary _____   10. seer _____

3 Phonology

3.1 Phonological Rules 1: English Past Tense

The examples in list I are representative of English verbs that form a regular past tense (i.e., their past tense form can be predicted). These past tense forms are shown in list II. Like the English plural morpheme, the English regular past tense morpheme has three variants: in this case, [t], [d], and [id].

Consider the data in lists I and II. (To facilitate your study, write the last sound of each word in the space provided.) Answer questions A–F, referring to distinctive features in your answers. (Instructions on writing rules are found in appendixes 1 and 2, and a list of distinctive features is found in appendix 4.)

	List I	Last sound of verb		List II	[t], [d], or [id]
1.	please	[z]		pleased	[d]
2.	grab	_____		grabbed	_____
3.	slam	_____		slammed	_____
4.	plan	_____		planned	_____
5.	fit	_____		fitted	_____
6.	fix	_____		fixed	_____
7.	pack	_____		packed	_____
8.	peep	_____		peeped	_____
9.	blend	_____		blended	_____
10.	seethe	_____		seethed	_____
11.	bomb	_____		bombed	_____
12.	hang	_____		hanged	_____
13.	fog	_____		fogged	_____
14.	flush	_____		flushed	_____
15.	knit	_____		knitted	_____
16.	fade	_____		faded	_____

Questions

A. In what environment does [t] occur? List the relevant segments and provide the distinctive features these segments have in common.

B. In what environment does [d] occur? List the relevant segments and provide the distinctive features these segments have in common.

C. In what environment does [ɨd] occur? List the relevant segments and provide the distinctive features these segments have in common.

D. What does the distribution (pattern of occurrence) of the past tense morpheme [t] have in common with the distribution of the plural morpheme [s]?

E. What does the distribution of past tense [d] have in common with the distribution of plural [z]?

F. What does the distribution of past tense [ɨd] have in common with the distribution of plural [ɨz]?

3.2 Phonological Rules 2: Korean [l] and [r]

In Korean, the sounds [l] and [r] are in complementary distribution. Examine the data below and answer the questions that follow.

		Korean word	English gloss
A.	1.	pal	"foot"
		paruy	"of the foot"
	2.	mul	"water"
		muruy	"of the water"
	3.	ssal	"rice"
		ssaruy	"of the rice"
	4.	saram	"person"
		saramuy	"of the person"
B.	5.	sul	"liquor"
		sultok	"liquor jug"
	6.	mul	"water"
		multok	"water jug"
	7.	ssal	"rice"
		ssaltok	"rice jug"
C.	8.	khal	"knife"
	9.	səul	"Seoul"
	10.	ilkop	"seven"
	11.	ipalsa	"barber"
	12.	məri	"head, hair"
	13.	rupi	"ruby"
	14.	ratio	"radio"

The data in 9–11 and 13–14 are from Fromkin and Rodman 1988, 116. There are two *s*'s in Korean, one transcribed here as *s* (lax) and the other as *ss* (fortis).

A. Given the data in set A (1–4), what is the form of the affix meaning "of (the)"?

B. What happens to [l] when the affix meaning "of (the)" is attached to the stem?

C. Given the data in set B (5–7), what is the form of the morpheme meaning "vessel for holding *X*" (glossed here as "jug")?

D. Considering both sets of data, A (1–4) and B (5–7), what generalizations can you make regarding the distribution of [l] and [r]? That is, where does [r] occur and where does [l] occur?

E. 1. Assume for the moment that [l] is basic. What would be the phonological rule necessary to derive [r]? (That is, $l \rightarrow r / \ldots ? \ldots$)

2. Assume for the moment that [r] is basic. What would be the phonological rule necessary to derive [l]? (That is, r → l /...?...)

3. Which rule, E-1 or E-2, would be preferable? That is, which rule is simpler, the rule deriving [l] from [r] or the rule deriving [r] from [l]?

F. Now consider the monomorphemic Korean words in set C (8–14). Does the generalization that you stated in question D hold true for these examples as well? If not, modify your generalization so that it accounts for these examples.

G. Is the phonological rule that you chose in question E-3 compatible with the generalization that you found in question F? If not, modify your rule so that it is.

H. Assuming the phonological rule that you developed in questions E–G, provide the underlying or basic representation of the words for "knife," "seven," and "ruby."

3.3 Phonological Rules 3: Tohono O'odham

In Tohono O'odham, a Native American language belonging to the Uto-Aztecan family, the sounds *ḍ* and *ṣ* are variants of the sounds *r* and *s*, respectively. That is, *r* and *s* are basic and *ḍ* and *ṣ* are derived. The *ḍ* is a voiced retroflex stop consonant, and the *ṣ* is a voiceless retroflex fricative. The complete list of Tohono O'odham speech sounds contains /p, t, k, ʔ, b, d, ḍ, g, h, ǰ, l, m, ñ, n, r, s, ṣ, w (v), y, č, a, i, ɨ, o, u, a:, i:, ɨ:, o:, u:/. The phonetic symbol *ɨ* is a high back unrounded vowel. The Tohono O'odham use the symbol *e* to write this sound since the Tohono O'odham language does not have a mid front vowel (English /ey/ and /ɛ/).

Examine the Tohono O'odham forms listed below and answer questions A–C. Instructions for writing phonological rules are found in appendixes 1 and 2.

	Tohono O'odham form	English gloss
1.	ʔaridt	"had a baby"
2.	ṣo:m	"sew"
3.	kuḍut	"bother"
4.	ṣɨ:piǰ	"younger brother, cousin"
5.	taḍaǰ	"his/her/its foot"
6.	ʔarik	"to be a baby"
7.	ʔɨḍapi	"gut, remove entrails"
8.	hi:kas	"cut"
9.	wuḍañ	"tie it!, rope it!"
10.	wuḍo	"untie"
11.	maṣad	"moon," "month"
12.	kuṣo	"back of neck"
13.	ṣoṣa	"mucous," "cried"
14.	si:s	"younger brother"
15.	bidk	"will be mud"
16.	wiḍut	"swing" (verb)
17.	ma:kis	"gift, something given"
18.	bisč	"sneeze"
19.	huḍuñ	"evening"
20.	kiriw	"shuck object"
21.	mɨriñ	"run!"
22.	ṣa:d	"herd, shoo"

A. What environment conditions the occurrence of the sounds ṣ and ḍ? That is, describe the phonological environments by listing the sounds whose occurrence is associated with the derived consonants ṣ and ḍ.

B. What distinctive features uniquely describe the natural class of sounds that condition the change of s to ṣ and r to ḍ?

C. Given the rule schema A → B / C＿＿D (see rule 3 in appendix 1), state the rule for the occurrence of ṣ and ḍ in Tohono O'odham. The change of s and r to ṣ and ḍ may be stated in terms of segments, as shown below; but the conditioning environment should be stated in terms of distinctive features. C and D in the schema are "placeholders" (variables). In any actual rule that conforms to the schema A → B / C＿＿D, one or the other of C and D may be empty. That is, the change from s and r to ṣ and ḍ may be conditioned (1) by something that occurs before s and r *and* something that occurs after (C and D), (2) by something that occurs before s and r (C only), or (3) by something that occurs after s and r (D only).

$$\begin{bmatrix} s \\ r \end{bmatrix} \rightarrow \begin{bmatrix} ṣ \\ ḍ \end{bmatrix}$$

3.4 Phonological Rules 4: Zoque

In the following forms from Zoque, a language spoken in Mexico, many of the symbols represent consonants whose properties can be predicted from the environment in which they occur. Study the forms and answer questions A–D. Instructions for writing phonological rules are found in appendixes 1 and 2.

The complete inventory of Zoque phonemes is /p, t, tˢ, tʸ, č, k, s, š, h, l, ʔ, m, n, ñ, ŋ, w, x, y, i, e, ə, a, o, u/.

	Zoque form	English gloss
1.	əŋdʸoʔys	"he got sleepy"
2.	kenba	"he sees"
3.	ndᶻin	"my pine"
4.	tʸətʸəy	"little"
5.	pama	"clothing"
6.	ñjehtˢu	"you cut"
7.	mingeʔtu	"he also came"
8.	mbama	"my clothing"
9.	ndʸuku	"you shot"
10.	ngengeʔtu	"I also saw it"
11.	petpa	"he sweeps"
12.	wixtu	"he walked"
13.	pəndaʔm	"men"
14.	myaŋdamu	"you went"
15.	nətʸuxu	"he's shouting"
16.	tˢehtˢu	"he cut brush"
17.	ñjinu	"he planted it"
18.	čehčaxu	"they cut it"
19.	anjiʔu	"goatee"
20.	čəknaʔču	"he frightened him"

A. You should be able to determine from the data that the sounds *b* and *p* are related phonologically. Given that *p* is the basic form, what is the environment that conditions the appearance of *b*? That is, list the sounds that condition the appearance of derived *b*.

B. List the distinctive feature(s) that characterize(s) the class of phonemes that condition the change of *p* to *b*.

C. You may have noticed that *p* is not the only consonant that has a variant in the environment described in question B. Identify the consonants that are subject to this rule. List the consonants that are the input to this rule on the left side of the arrow, and list the corresponding derived consonants on the right side of the arrow.

p → b

D. Write the rule for Zoque discussed in question C using the rule schema A → B / C _____ D. Using distinctive feature notation, describe the natural class of consonants that are subject to the rule as A, indicate the feature(s) that result from the application of the rule as B, and write the conditioning environment from question B as C and D.

3.5 Phonological Rules 5: Japanese

Below are two lists of Japanese verb forms. List I consists of the base forms of verbs to which various affixes can be attached. List II consists of base forms to which the suffix *-te* has been added. This morpheme indicates continuous/progressive action, as in *Ima ame ga futte imasu* "It's raining now." Examine the data in the two lists and answer the questions that follow.

List I		List II
Japanese base form	English gloss	Japanese *-te* form
1. tabe-	"eat"	tabete
2. yob-	"call"	yonde
3. shin-	"die"	shinde
4. kak-	"write"	kaite
5. yom-	"read"	yonde
6. mi-	"see"	mite
7. asob-	"play"	asonde
8. tob-	"fly"	tonde
9. aruk-	"walk"	aruite
10. nom-	"drink"	nonde

Questions

A. For the purposes of this exercise, assume that *-te* is attached to the base forms in list I. Questions A-1 through A-4 ask you to propose phonological rules to account for the forms in list II. That is, they ask you to show how, with a small number of rules, the phonological alternations that the base forms and the suffix *-te* undergo during the suffixation process can be accounted for.

See appendix 1 for instructions on how to write informal phonological rules. The answer to question A-1 is given to illustrate the form the rules should take in this exercise.

1. Write the rule that accounts for the alternation in the forms given in example 3.

   Answer

   Rule 1: t → d / $\begin{bmatrix} \text{voiced} \\ \text{consonantal} \end{bmatrix}$ ____

   or t → [+voiced] / [+voiced, +consonantal] ____

2. Write the rule that accounts for the alternations in examples 4 and 9.

   Rule 2:

3. To account for the list II forms in examples 5 and 10, two rules are needed. one of which has already been stated as rule 1. Write a second rule that, when applied in combination with rule 1, will produce the list II forms in examples 5 and 10. Does the order in which these rules apply make any difference?

   Rule 3:

4. Examples 2, 7, and 8 introduce yet another complication in the phonology of Japanese. They illustrate again that rules in a grammar may (or must) be ordered with respect to each other. Only one additional rule needs to be added to your list of rules if the output of this rule is allowed to "feed into" the rules you have already written. Write this rule as rule 4.

   Rule 4:

B. List the rules that are needed to derive each of the forms given in list II, ordering them where necessary. That is, list them in the order in which they must apply to derive the correct forms. Use the numbers to refer to the rules.

   1. tabete   _____

   2. yonde   _____

   3. shinde   _____

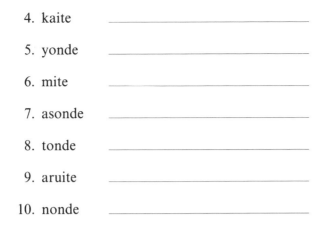

4. kaite   ——————————————

5. yonde   ——————————————

6. mite   ——————————————

7. asonde   ——————————————

8. tonde   ——————————————

9. aruite   ——————————————

10. nonde   ——————————————

C. Based on rules 1–4, what would you guess to be the *-te* form for the base *nug-*? Given the data in lists I and II, there are two possible answers. Why is this so? (Hint: *g* is like *k* in some respects, but like *d* and *b* in others.) Discuss which of the rules 1–4 may be potentially applicable (with some adjustments).

D. Can the base form of *erande* "be choosing" be predicted by rules 1–4? Why or why not?

3.6 Phonological Rules 6: Japanese

Examine the following data from Japanese and answer the questions.

	Japanese form	English gloss
1.	aketa	"opened"
2.	akerareta	"was opened"
3.	akesaseta	"caused to open"
4.	akesaserareta	"was caused to open"
5.	tabeta	"ate"
6.	taberareta	"was eaten"
7.	tabesaseta	"caused to eat"
8.	tabesaserareta	"was caused to eat"
9.	yonda	"read" (past)
10.	yomareta	"was read"
11.	yomaseta	"caused to read"
12.	yomaserareta	"was caused to read"
13.	tonda	"flew"
14.	tobareta	"was flown"
15.	tobaseta	"caused to fly"
16.	tobaserareta	"was caused to fly"
17.	ataeta	"awarded"
18.	ataerareta	"was awarded"
19.	ataesaseta	"caused to award"
20.	ataesaserareta	"was caused to award"
21.	eranda	"chose"
22.	erabareta	"was chosen"
23.	erabaseta	"caused to choose"
24.	erabaserareta	"was caused to choose"

A. What are the Japanese morphemes that correspond to each of the following words in English?

       Japanese morpheme   English word

  1. _____   open

  2. _____   eat

  3. _____   read

  4. _____   fly

  5. _____   award

  6. _____   choose

B. 1. The past tense suffix appears in two forms. What are they?

    2. Write an informal phonological rule that changes one form of the suffix into the other. Use the correct distinctive feature(s) in stating the rule (see appendix 2). (Hint: Assume *ta* is basic.)

C. 1. The causative suffix appears in two forms. What are they?

    2. What conditions determine which form of the suffix occurs?

D. 1. The passive suffix appears in two forms. What are they?

    2. What conditions determine which form of the suffix occurs?

    3. Write a phonological rule that relates the two forms of the suffix. Use the correct distinctive feature(s) in stating the rule (see appendix 2).

E. Is there any similarity between the causative and passive affixes? (Examine your responses to questions C-2 and D-2.)

F. Is there any similarity between the continuative/progressive -te form of the verb analyzed in exercise 3.5 and the past tense form?

3.7 Special Topic 1: Phonetic Variation (English /t/)

The phoneme /t/ in English has six allophones, whose conditioning environments are summarized in the following table. (See *Linguistics*, pp. 82–85.) After examining the table, answer questions A and B.

Articulatory description	Phonetic symbol	Conditioning environment	Example words
Released, aspirated	[tʰ]	when syllable-initial	tin [tʰɪn]
Unreleased, preglottalized	[ʔt]	word-final, after a vowel	kit [kʰɪʔt]
Glottal stop	[ʔ]	before a syllabic *n*	kitten [kʰɪʔn̩]
Flap	[D]	between vowels, when the first vowel is stressed (approximate environment)	pitted [pʰɪDɨd]
Alveopalatal stop	[ť]	syllable-initial before *r*	truck [ťrʌk]
Released, unaspirated	[t]	when the above conditions are not met first	stint [stɪnt]

Questions

A. Identify the variant of /t/ in each word below. For some dialects of English the "conditioning environments" described in the table are not descriptively adequate and require modification. Check to see if in your dialect any adjustments need to be made in the environments.

Word	Variant of /t/	Conditioning environment
1. after	_____	_____
2. beautiful	_____	_____
3. embitter	_____	_____

4. that   _____   _____

5. cotton   _____   _____

6. cent   _____   _____

7. Burt   _____   _____

8. built   _____   _____

9. butler   _____   _____

10. Burton   _____   _____

11. substance _____   _____

12. atoms   _____   _____

13. result   _____   _____

14. phonetics _____   _____

15. revolt   _____   _____

16. antler   _____   _____

17. settler   _____   _____

18. try   _____   _____

19. attitude   _____   _____

20. article   _____   _____

B. In the spaces provided, write your rules for changing /t/ to [tʰ], [ʔt], [ʔ], [D], [t̆], and [t], respectively. You may want to refer to appendix 1 for instructions on how to write phonological rules.

1.

2.

3.

4.

5.

6.

3.8 Special Topic 2: Phonetic Variation (French Vowels)

Examine the following data from French and answer questions A–D. (Assume that /e/ ~ /ɛ/, /ö/ ~ /ɔ̈/, and /o/ ~ /ɔ/ form three pairs of allophones.)

French form		English gloss
1. /bote/	beauté	"beauty"
2. /bɛl/	belle	"beautiful"
3. /pö/	peu	"small amount"
4. /pɔ̈r/	peur	"fear"
5. /mo/	mot	"word"
6. /mɔr/	mort	"death"

Questions

A. In what environment do /e/, /ö/, and /o/ occur? (Hint: Look at syllable structure.)

B. In what environment do /ɛ/, /ɔ̈/, and /ɔ/ occur? (Hint: Again, look at syllable structure.)

C. According to the following chart, what single feature distinguishes /e/, /ö/, and /o/ from /ɛ/, /ɔ̈/, and /ɔ/?

	e	ɛ	ö	ɔ̈	o	ɔ
Back	−	−	−	−	+	+
Round	−	−	+	+	+	+
Tense	+	−	+	−	+	−

D. The word *bête* "beast" is pronounced [bɛt]. What role do you think the symbol ˆ is playing here? (Hint: Note that the final orthographic *e* is not pronounced. Also, an alternative spelling in an earlier stage of French was *bette*.)

3.9 Special Topic 3: Liaison (French)

Examine the data in list I and answer question A; then consult the data in list II in order to answer questions B–E.

List I

French orthography	Pronunciation	English gloss
1. petit	[pəti]	"little"
2. vous	[vu]	"you"
3. premier	[prəmye]	"first"
4. comment	[kɔmã]	"(adv.) how"
5. nous	[nu]	"we"
6. mangez	[mãže]	"(you pl.) eat"

List II

French orthography	Pronunciation	English gloss
1. petit morceau	[pətimɔrso]	"little bit"
2. petit avion	[pətitavyɔ̃]	"little airplane"
3. vous avez	[vuzave]	"you have"
4. vous buvez	[vubüve]	"you are drinking"
5. premier étage	[prəmyɛretaž]	"first floor"
6. premier garçon	[prəmyegarsɔ̃]	"first boy"
7. comment allez-vous	[kɔmãtalevu]	"how are you (lit. going)?"
8. comment venez-vous	[kɔmãvənevu]	"how are you coming?"
9. nous avons	[nuzavɔ̃]	"we have"
10. nous buvons	[nubüvɔ̃]	"we are drinking"
11. mangez-en	[mãžezã]	"(you pl.) eat some (of it)"
12. mangez-la (la pomme)	[mãžela]	"(you pl.) eat it (the apple)"

A. Compare the orthographic representations in list I with the phonetic representations ("Pronunciation" column); ignore the vowels. How do the phonetic representations consistently differ from the orthographic ones?

B. How do the data in list I differ from the data in list II?

C. Describe what appears to be conditioning the change(s) that you noted in question B.

D. On the basis of your hypothesis in question C, provide the *underlying* representations for the words in list I (i.e., the phonemic representation indicated by / /). (See *Linguistics*, pp. 77–80.)

1. petit   _____

2. vous   _____

3. premier   _____

4. comment   _____

5. nous   _____

6. mangez   _____

E. Provide evidence to support your answer in question D.

4 Syntax

Name

Section

4.1 English Syntax 1: Simple Phrase Structure Rules

Consider the following two sets of phrase structure rules for English, and answer questions A–D. You may find it helpful to review *Linguistics*, pp. 187–192.

Phrase structure rules

Set I

1. S → NP Aux VP
2. NP → Art N PP
3. PP → P NP
4. VP → V NP
5. NP → Art N PP
6. PP → P NP
7. NP → Art N

Set II

1. S → NP Aux VP
2. NP → Art N
3. VP → V NP PP
4. NP → Art N
5. PP → P NP
6. NP → Art N

Questions

A. Draw the phrase structure tree that is defined by applying the phrase structure rules 1–7 in set I. Be sure to apply the rules in the order they are given. (In other words, apply rule 1; then apply rule 2 to the output of rule 1; and so forth.)

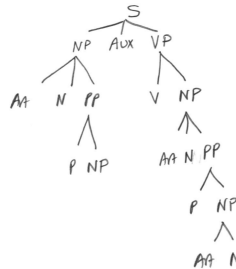

B. Give an appropriate sentence for the tree you have drawn in question A.

The gorilla above the path will hurl his banana beside the elephant.

C. Draw the phrase structure tree that is defined by applying the phrase structure rules 1–6 in set II, in the order they are given.

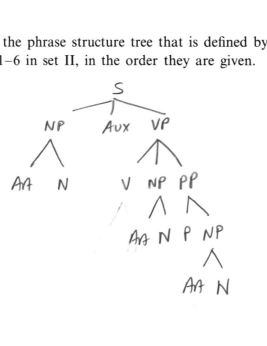

D. Give an appropriate sentence for the tree you have drawn in question C.

An assassin can kill the president with a toothpick.

Name _____

Section _____

4.2 English Syntax 2: Simple NPs, VPs, and PPs

Provide the following tree structures. To do so, you may find it helpful to review *Linguistics*, pp. 187–192.

Questions

A. Draw a tree structure for each of the following noun phrases:

1. the boy in the tree

2. a sign on the door

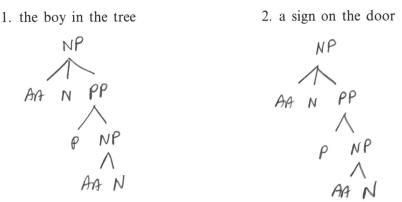

B. Draw a tree structure for each of the following verb phrases:

1. hit the ball

2. hammered the nail into the wall

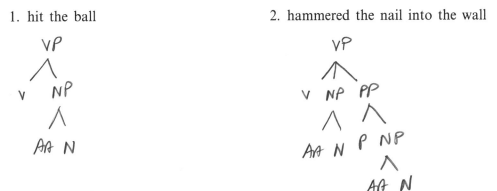

C. Draw a tree structure for each of the following prepositional phrases:

1. up the tree in the yard

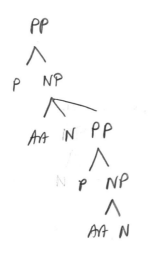

2. on the desk near the window

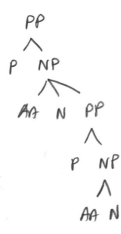

D. Draw a tree structure for each of the following sentences:

1. The boy in the tree near the house threw the ball into the yard.

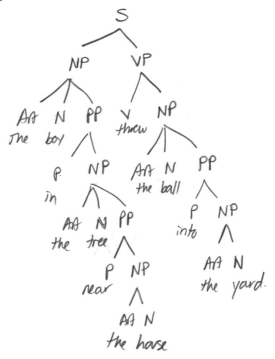

? 2. The professor put the book about linguistics on the table near the podium.

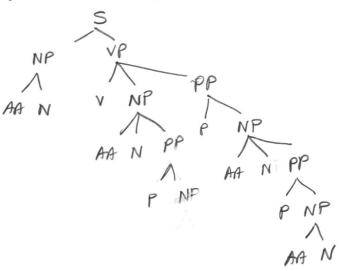

4.3 English Syntax 3: Tree Terminology

Examine the following tree structure and answer questions A–G. You may find it helpful to review *Linguistics*, pp. 157–162 and 187–192.

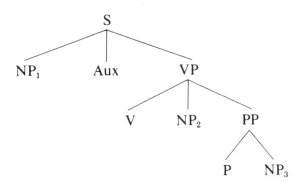

Questions

A. Are NP$_2$ and NP$_3$ sisters? Why or why not?

No, because NP$_2$ is a daughter of VP and NP$_3$ is a daughter of PP.

B. Are Aux and VP sisters? Why or why not?

yes, because they are both daughters of S.

C. Do NP₁ and Aux form a single constituent? Why or why not?

No, because they are diffemt nodes.

D. Do P and NP₃ form a single constituent? Why or why not?

Yes, because they are daughters of a phrase.

E. Which NP is the subject? How do you know?

NP₁, because it precedes the auxiliary and is dominated by S.

F. Which NP is the direct object? How do you know?

NP₂, because it is dominated by VP.

G. Give the simplest phrase structure rules that will generate the above tree. (Consult appendix 5 for a list of some phrase structure rules for English.)

1. S → NP Aux VP
2. VP → V NP PP
3. PP → P NP

Name _____

Section _____

4.4 English Syntax 4: Ill-Formed Trees

The tree structures 1–8 are all ill formed. That is, there is no combination of phrase structure rules or transformations that will generate any of them. Study the trees and answer the question.

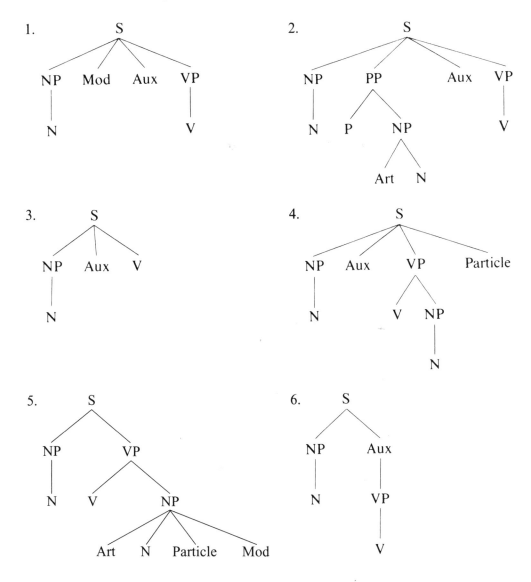

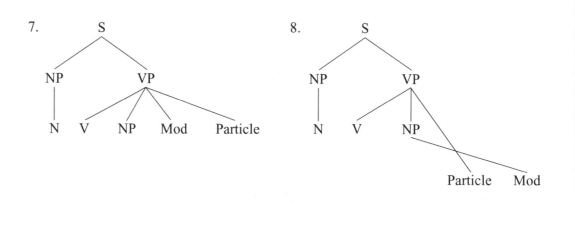

Question

For each tree, state what the problem is (i.e., why it cannot be generated by the phrase structure rules) and correct it when possible *without* altering the linear order of any of the nodes. A list of some of the phrase structure rules for English is given in appendix 5. You may find it helpful to review *Linguistics*, pp. 187–192.

1.

2.

3.

4.

5.

6.

7.

8.

4.5 English Syntax 5: Tree and Sentence Matching

Below are three sentences and four structures. Match each structure with a sentence and then answer questions A–E.

1. The doctor called the patient up on the phone.
2. John saw a girl with a telescope.
3. The boy's father, who works at IBM, plays chess.

Structure I

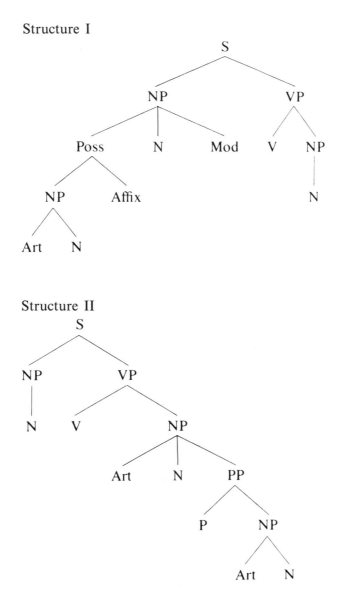

Structure II

Structure III

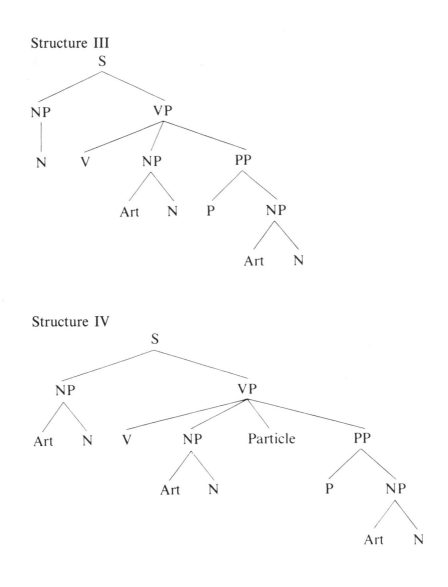

Structure IV

Questions

A. Why can three sentences be associated with four structures in the above examples? That is, why are the sentences 1, 2, and 3 associated with four structures?

B. One of the sentences is the output of a transformation discussed in chapter 5 of *Linguistics*. Which sentence is it? (Hint: Review *Linguistics*, pp. 169–183.)

C. Which transformation is involved in generating the sentence that is your answer to question B?

D. What is the input sentence for the transformation mentioned in question C?

E. What is the tree structure for the sentence you have written in answer to question D? That is, what is the input tree for the transformation mentioned in question C?

4.6 English Syntax 6: Transformations

Study the following sentence and answer questions A–D. It will be helpful to review *Linguistics*, pp. 141–150, 153–154, 176–183.

1. Can she wash the shoes off?

Questions

A. What is the underlying (basic) sentence for sentence 1?

2.

B. What two syntactic rules are needed to transform sentence 2 into sentence 1?

C. Draw the tree structure for sentence 1.

D. Draw the tree structure for the input (basic) sentence 2.

4.7 English Syntax 7: Possessive NP with a PP

In this exercise you will be asked to draw the tree structure for the following sentence:

The baby on the doctor's lap's mother will visit her brother.

Considering the following questions first will help you in determining the correct tree structure. It will also be helpful to review *Linguistics*, pp. 195–197.

1. Who will "visit her brother"?
2. What would be an appropriate tag question for the sentence? (On tag questions, see *Linguistics*, pp. 147–150, 155.)
3. Whose mother is it?
4. Where is the baby?
5. What phrase structure rules will be required to generate the subject constituent of the sentence? To answer this question, look for items like prepositions, articles, and possessive affixes.

Question

Provide the tree structure for the example sentence.

4.8 English Syntax 8: Verb-Particle versus Verb-PP Structure

Each of the sentences 1–6 involves either a verb+particle followed by a noun phrase (structure I) or a verb followed by a prepositional phrase (structure II).

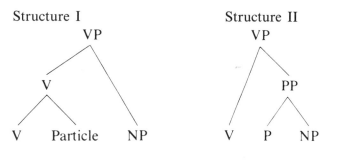

1. John ran into the street.
2. Paul called up Tim.
3. The child slipped into the closet.
4. I calmed down the clerk.
5. The student filled in the blanks.
6. Deer can leap over the fence.

Below you will be asked to determine which of the two structures is relevant for each sentence. To make this determination, use the following constituent structure tests:

Cleft construction (see *Linguistics*, pp. 163–165)

It is/was *X* that *Y*.

A single constituent substitutes for *X* in this construction. For example, consider the sentence *Sally threw out the garbage*. Assume that *out the garbage* is a single constituent (i.e., an instance of structure II). If this assumption is correct, then *out the garbage* should be able to substitute for *X* in the cleft construction to produce a grammatical sentence. However, *It was out the garbage that Sally threw* is not a grammatical sentence, indicating that *out the garbage* is not a single constituent and consequently that the VP structure for *threw out the garbage* is I, not II.

Conjunction (see *Linguistics*, pp. 165–166)

X and *Y*

X and *Y* must be of the same category (as for instance in *He threw the pen* [$_{PP}$ *through the window*] *and* [$_{PP}$ *onto the floor*]). For example, if *out the garbage* is a PP in *Sally threw out the garbage*, then it should be possible to conjoin another PP—say, *into the can*—with it. But the resulting sentence is ungrammatical: **Sally threw out the garbage and into the can*. Conclusion: *out the garbage* is not a PP. The relevant structure for the VP is again shown to be I, not II.

Particle Movement transformation (see *Linguistics*, pp. 183–187)

SD: *X* – V – Particle – NP – *Y*
     1   2   3   4   5 ⇒
SC: 1   2   ∅   4 + 3   5
            (or: V NP + Particle)

If the cleft and conjunction tests have failed to yield a grammatical sentence, then this predicts that the sentence in question involves an instance of the verb + particle construction (structure I) and that the Particle Movement transformation should be able to apply. In our example, applying Particle Movement to *Sally threw out the garbage* indeed produces a grammatical sentence (*Sally threw the garbage out*), indicating again that *threw out the garbage* is an instance of structure I.

Questions

Apply the three constituent structure tests to sentences 1–6 to determine which structure (I or II) is correct for each one. In the spaces provided, state which structure is correct for each sentence and give the evidence for your answer (i.e., mention the results of the tests).

1.

    Cleft:

    Conjunction:

    Particle Movement:

2.

    Cleft:

    Conjunction:

    Particle Movement:

3.

    Cleft:

    Conjunction:

    Particle Movement:

4.

    Cleft:

    Conjunction:

    Particle Movement:

5.

    Cleft:

    Conjunction:

    Particle Movement:

6.

    Cleft:

    Conjunction:

    Particle Movement:

Below are more examples (7–12) for extra practice.

7. The athlete worked out the problem.
8. She washed off her shoes.
9. The lady fell down the stairs.
10. She let down her hair.
11. He helped out the child.
12. He walked out the door.

4.9 English Syntax 9: S-Adverbs versus VP-Adverbs

In chapter 5 of *Linguistics* a distinction is made between S-adverbs and VP-adverbs (see pp. 185–187). S-adverbs have scope over (i.e., modify) the entire sentence; VP-adverbs have scope over (i.e., modify) just the VP. A test for determining whether an adverb is an S-adverb or a VP-adverb is whether it can occur in the X position in

It is/was X the case that Y.

If it can, then it is an S-adverb. For example, *surely*, which is an S-adverb, can substitute for X (*It is surely the case that Paula will succeed*), whereas *quickly*, which is not an S-adverb, cannot (**It is quickly the case that Paula will succeed*).
Consider the following examples and answer questions A–D.

1a. John listened to the music *intently*.
 b. John listened to the music *finally*.

2a. Mary speaks French *fluently*.
 b. Mary speaks French *happily*.

3a. Paul taunted her *unfortunately*.
 b. Paul taunted her *unjustly*.

Questions

A. Which adverbs are S-adverbs? Provide evidence to support your decisions (i.e., provide the relevant example sentences). (Caution: Be sure that the sense of the original sentence has not been altered in the "test" sentence.)

B. Which adverbs are VP-adverbs? Provide evidence to support your decisions.

C. At least one adverb is ambiguous with respect to its status (i.e., it can be either an S-adverb or a VP-adverb). Which adverb(s) do you consider ambiguous and why?

D. Determine the status of the following adverbs (i.e., whether each one is an S-adverb or a VP-adverb), providing relevant example sentences to support your decisions.

1. fortunately

2. forcibly

3. openly

4. certainly

4.10 English Syntax 10: Arguing for Syntactic Structure

Consider the following sentence and answer the questions below:

The TA who is entering the room will pass out the exam at the door.

Questions

A. Draw a tree structure for the example sentence given above.

B. Determine five pieces of evidence that support the structure you have drawn in question A. For example, you can use the following constructions as evidence: yes/no questions (to test for the subject constituent), clefts and conjunctions (to test for the structure of the VP), negative placement, and tag questions.

Provide your five pieces of evidence in the answer sections labeled 1–5. In each case, give the following information in the spaces labeled a–d:

a. State what you are trying to show (e.g., that X is the subject constituent).

b. Provide example sentence(s) (e.g., example(s) of yes/no questions).

c. State whether the example sentence passes or fails the test.

d. State the significance of the results you found in part c.

1. a.

   b.

   c.

   d.

2. a.

   b.

   c.

   d.

3. a.

b.

c.

d.

4. a.

b.

c.

d.

5. a.

b.

c.

d.

4.11 Simple Sentences 1: German

Study the German sentences 1–25 and answer the questions that follow.

The German sentences are all in the perfective tense, which corresponds to the simple past in English: for example, *hat gemacht* "made." In English the perfective is made up of the auxiliary verb *have* and the past participle of the main verb: for example, *John has eaten.* In German the perfective is also made up of an auxiliary verb and the past participle of the main verb, but German uses two different auxiliary verbs: *haben* "to have" and *sein* "to be." The auxiliary verb *sein*, which appears in its third person singular form *ist* in this exercise, is used when the main verb refers to "motion" or a "change in state"; otherwise, the auxiliary verb is *haben.* In sentence 3, for example, the verb *fahren* "to travel," which indicates motion, appears in its third person singular perfective form with auxiliary *sein: ist gefahren.*

1. Er hat gestern eine Bemerkung gemacht.
   "He made a remark yesterday."
2. Gestern hat er eine Bemerkung gemacht.
   "Yesterday he made a remark."
3. Sie ist langsam in die Stadt gefahren.
   "She traveled into the city slowly."
4. Er hat nicht langsam gesprochen.
   "He didn't speak slowly."
5. Langsam ist sie in die Stadt gefahren.
   "Slowly she traveled into the city."
6. Gestern ist sie nicht in die Stadt gefahren.
   "Yesterday she didn't travel into the city."
7. Gefahren ist der Mann in die Stadt.
   "The man traveled into the city."
8. Den Mann hat er nicht gesehen.
   "He didn't see the man."
9. Gesehen hat eine Frau einen Mann.
   "A woman saw a man."
10. Eine Frau hat ein Mann gesehen.
    "A man saw a woman."
11. Sie hat die Bemerkung nicht gemacht.
    "She didn't make the remark."
12. Ein Mann ist nicht gegangen.
    "A man didn't go."

13. Er hat sie nicht gesehen.
    "He didn't see her."
14. Der Mann hat die Frau nicht gesehen.
    "The man didn't see the woman."
15. Der Mann ist mit der Frau gestern in die Stadt gefahren.
    "The man traveled into the city yesterday with the woman."
16. Mit der Frau ist der Mann gestern in die Stadt gefahren.
    Same as 15
17. Gestern ist der Mann mit der Frau in die Stadt gefahren.
    Same as 15
18. In die Stadt ist der Mann mit der Frau gestern gefahren.
    Same as 15
19. Sie hat keine Bemerkung gemacht.
    "She didn't make a remark."
20. Keine Bemerkung hat sie gemacht.
    Same as 19
21. Er hat die Bemerkung nicht gemacht.
    "He didn't make the remark."
22. Sie hat ihn nicht gesehen.
    "She didn't see him."
23. Die Frau hat keine Bemerkung gemacht.
    "The woman didn't make a remark."
24. Er hat keine Frau gesehen.
    "He didn't see a woman."
25. Keinen Mann hat sie gesehen.
    "She didn't see a man."

Questions

A. In German the nominative case is generally used to mark the subject of the sentence, whereas the accusative case is used to mark objects. Below, list the corresponding nominative-accusative forms that occur in this exercise. The parentheses indicate words that are not found in the data. Enter what you would predict to be the correct German forms.

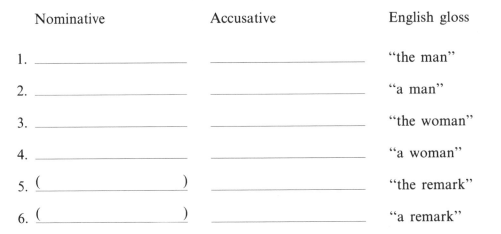

Nominative	Accusative	English gloss
1. _____	_____	"the man"
2. _____	_____	"a man"
3. _____	_____	"the woman"
4. _____	_____	"a woman"
5. (_____)	_____	"the remark"
6. (_____)	_____	"a remark"

7. _____   _____   "he/him"

8. _____   _____   "she/her"

B. What word in German corresponds most closely to the English word *not* (*-n't*)?

C. The overall meaning of sentences 15–18 is the same, although extra emphasis is placed on the word or phrase that is in sentence-initial position. What general property of German word order is reflected in sentences 15–18 that is also reflected in all of the other sentences in this exercise? That is, in spite of the variation in the sentences, what remains constant? Discuss particular examples to illustrate your points.

D. *Bonus*. The German system of negation is quite different from that of Modern English in a particular feature that is illustrated in the data. Note that the word *nicht* does not appear in all of the sentences that are translated into negative sentences in English. What is another form of the negative in German, and what are the conditions under which this form appears?

4.12 Simple Sentences 2: Tamil

Examine the following sentences from Tamil, a Dravidian language spoken in India, and answer the questions that follow.

1a. Na:n mi:nai va:nkukire:n.
 b. Mi:nai va:nkukire:n.
 c. Mi:nai na:n va:nkukire:n.
 "I buy the fish."

2a. Ma:lukira:n.
 b. Avan ma:lukira:n.
 "He dies."

3a. Unnai pa:rkire:n.
 b. Na:n unnai pa:rkire:n.
 "I see you."

4a. Vilukira:y.
 b. Ni: vilukira:y.
 "You fall."

5a. Karro:n a:ntiyai pa:rkira:n. *(S DO V (s))*
 b. A:ntiyai pa:rkira:n karro:n. *(DO V(s) S)*
 "The teacher sees the monk."

6. Avan va:nkukira:n. *(S V–S)*
 "He buys."

7a. Avanai vaikire:n. *(DO V–S)*
 b. Vaikire:n avanai na:n. *(V–S DO S)*
 c. Avanai vaikire:n na:n. *(DO V–S S)*
 "I scold him."

8a. Ni: ennai vaikira:y. *(S DO V–S)*
 b. Vaikira:y ennai. *(V–S DO)*
 "You scold me."

9a. Manitan unnai vaikira:n. *(S DO V)*
 b. Manitan vaikira:n unnai. *(S V DO)*
 "The man scolds you."

10. Vaikira:n avanai. *(V–S DO)*
 "He scolds him."

11. Avan manitanai vaikira:n.
(S, DO, V markers above)
   "He scolds the man."

12a. Karro:n ennai pa:rkira:n.
   (S, DO, V markers above)
   b. Pa:rkira:n ennai karro:n.
   (V, DO, S markers above)
   "The teacher sees me."

Questions

A. Isolate the Tamil morphemes, entering them in the spaces below. The parentheses indicate words that are not found in the data. Enter what you would predict to be the correct Tamil forms.

1. Verb

Tamil form	English gloss
a. va:nku	"buy"
b. ma:lu	"die"
c. pa:r	"see"
d. vilu	"fall"
e. vai	"scold"
f. -kir-	"present tense morpheme"

2. Nouns

Subject form	Object form	English gloss
a. manitan	manitanai	"man"
b. korro:n	(karro:nai)	"teacher"
c. (mi:n)	mi:nai	"fish"
d. (antiy)	antiyai	"monk"

3. Pronouns

Subject form (free)	Subject form (bound)	English gloss
a. na:n	-e:n	"I"
b. ni:	-a:y	"you"
c. avan	-a:n	"he"

	Object form (free)	English gloss
d.	_enrai_	"me"
e.	_unnrai_	"you"
f.	_avanai_	"him"

B. How are grammatical relations (subject, object) indicated in Tamil?

The object form is indicated by the suffix "-ai."

C. Discuss the role of word order (if any) in Tamil. Is it necessary to examine word order to determine the direct object in Tamil? Explain.

4.13 Simple Sentences 3: Tohono O'odham

Study the Tohono O'odham sentences 1–25 and answer the questions that follow.

The *g* before some of the words is a definite article that is close (though not identical) in meaning to the English word *the*. It never appears in sentence-initial position. The hyphen, -, indicates the sequence "prefix-stem." The asterisk, *, as usual indicates an ungrammatical sentence.

The *ñ* is an alveopalatal nasal; *č* is a voiceless alveopalatal affricate; ' is a glottal stop; *ḍ* is a voiced retroflex stop; orthographic *e* is a high back unrounded vowel (phonetically [ɨ]). A vowel with a colon after it (*i:*) is long. You may wish to consult appendix 3 for more information about the sounds in this exercise, though an exact understanding of them is not necessary to complete it successfully.

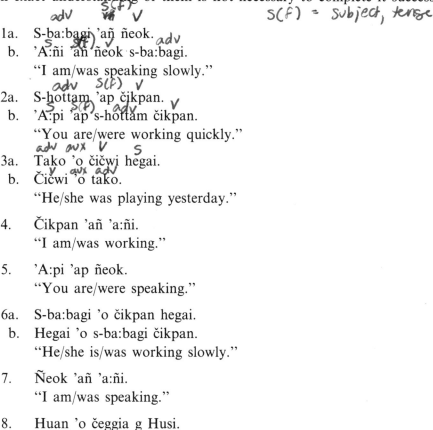

1a. S-ba:bagi 'añ ñeok.
 b. 'A:ñi 'añ ñeok s-ba:bagi.
 "I am/was speaking slowly."

2a. S-hottam 'ap čikpan.
 b. 'A:pi 'ap s-hottam čikpan.
 "You are/were working quickly."

3a. Tako 'o čičwi hegai.
 b. Čičwi 'o tako.
 "He/she was playing yesterday."

4. Čikpan 'añ 'a:ñi.
 "I am/was working."

5. 'A:pi 'ap ñeok.
 "You are/were speaking."

6a. S-ba:bagi 'o čikpan hegai.
 b. Hegai 'o s-ba:bagi čikpan.
 "He/she is/was working slowly."

7. Ñeok 'añ 'a:ñi.
 "I am/was speaking."

8. Huan 'o čeggia g Husi.
 "John is/was fighting Joe."   *or*
 "Joe is/was fighting John."

9. Husi 'o g Huan čeggia.
"John is/was fighting Joe." *or*
"Joe is/was fighting John."

10. M-čeggia 'o g Huan.
"John is/was fighting you."

11. Huan 'o ñ-čeggia.
"John is/was fighting me."

12. Čeggia 'o g Husi g Huan.
"Joe is/was fighting John." *or*
"John is/was fighting Joe."

13. Mi:stol 'o ko:ṣ.
"The cat is/was sleeping."

14a. 'A:ñi 'añ meḍ.
   b. Meḍ 'añ.
   "I am/was running."

15. Huan 'o čendad g Mali:ya.
"John is/was kissing Mary." *or*
"Mary is/was kissing John."

16. Mali:ya 'o čendad g Huan.
"John is/was kissing Mary." *or*
"Mary is/was kissing John."

17a. Čeoǰ 'o 'a:ñi ñ-čeggia.
   b. Ñ-čeggia 'o g čeoǰ 'a:ñi.
   "The boy is/was fighting me."

18a. Tako 'o g čeoǰ ñ-čeggia.
   b. Ñ-čeggia 'o g čeoǰ 'a:ñi tako.
   "The boy is/was fighting me yesterday."

19a. Mali:ya 'o m-čendad 'a:pi.
   b. 'A:pi 'o m-čendad g Mali:ya.
   "Mary is/was kissing you."

20a. Gogs 'o hegai huhu'id.
   b. Huhu'id 'o g gogs hegai.
   "The dog is/was chasing it/him/her."

21. M-huhu'id 'o g gogs.
"The dog is chasing you."

22. 'A:ñi 'añ g gogs huhu'id.
"I am/was chasing the dog."

23a. *Husi g Huan 'o čeggia.
   b. *Čeggia g Husi g Huan 'o.
   c. *'O čeggia g Husi g Huan.

24a. *Meḍ 'a:ñi 'añ.
   b. *'A:ni meḍ 'añ.

25a. *Čikpan s-hottam 'ap.
  b. *S-hottam čikpan 'ap.

Questions

A. Write the Tohono O'odham verb morphemes corresponding to the English glosses in the spaces provided.

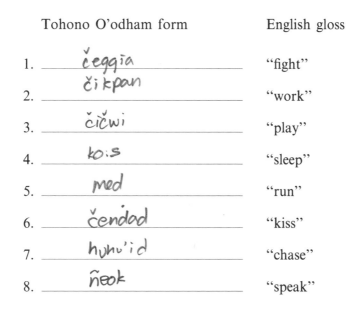

Tohono O'odham form	English gloss
1. čeggia	"fight"
2. čikpan	"work"
3. čičwi	"play"
4. ko:s	"sleep"
5. med	"run"
6. čendad	"kiss"
7. huhu'id	"chase"
8. ñeok	"speak"

B. Tohono O'odham has auxiliary elements that mark person as well as tense/aspect. The auxiliary elements appearing in this exercise are translated into English as "*Y* is/was V-ing," where *Y* is some person or animal and V stands for the verb. List these elements in the spaces provided below.

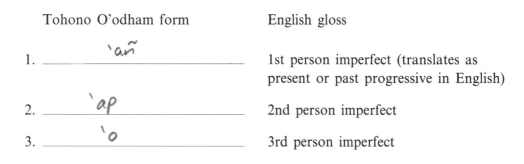

Tohono O'odham form	English gloss
1. 'añ	1st person imperfect (translates as present or past progressive in English)
2. 'ap	2nd person imperfect
3. 'o	3rd person imperfect

C. List the Tohono O'odham nouns used in this exercise.

Tohono O'odham form	English gloss
1.	"John" (Juan)
2.	"cat"

3. _____ "boy"

4. _____ "Joe" (Jose)

5. _____ "Mary"

6. _____ "dog"

D. In sentence 13 you had to determine which word meant "cat." How did you make your decision? That is, what evidence did you bring to bear on your decision?

E. List the Tohono O'odham independent pronouns used in the example sentences.

Tohono O'odham form   English gloss

1. _____ "I/me"

2. _____ "he him, she/her, it"

3. _____ "you"

F. Give one or two interesting properties of the Tohono O'odham independent pronouns.

G. List the Tohono O'odham adverbs corresponding to the English glosses.

Tohono O'odham form   English gloss

1. _____   "slowly"

2. _____   "quickly"

3. _____   "yesterday"

H. How are grammatical relations (subject, object) indicated in Tohono O'odham? For example, does word order play a role in determining grammatical relations? Does morphology play a role?

No diff between subj + obj pronouns. No word order.
Object markers for 1st + 2nd person, not 3rd.

I. What obligatory condition on word order is true for Tohono O'odham? Be sure to take into account the ungrammatical sentences 23–25.

Aux verb must be in 2nd position

4.14 Simple Sentences 4: Yaqui

Yaqui is a member of the Uto-Aztecan language family and is still spoken in the Mexican state of Sonora and in southern Arizona. Examine the data below and answer the questions that follow. Italicization of the English pronoun in a translation indicates that the Yaqui pronoun is interpreted as emphatic.

	Yaqui form	English gloss
1.	Vempo uka karita veetak.	"*They* burned the house."
2.	Aapo apo'ik vichak.	"*He* saw him (someone else)."
3.	Aapo uka vachita itou nenkak.	"*He* sold the corn to us."
4.	Inepo siika.	"I left."
5.	Siikane.	"I left."
6.	Tuukate tekipanoak.	"We worked yesterday."
7.	Uka ili'uusitam aniak.	"They helped the child."
8.	Siikate.	"We left."
9.	Maria abʷisek.	"Mary grabbed it."
10.	Maria ambʷisek.	"Mary grabbed them."
11.	Empo nee aniak.	"*You* helped *me*."
12.	Peo haivu kutam chuktak.	"Pete already chopped wood."
13.	Peo haivu amchuktak.	"Pete already chopped them."
14.	*Peo amhaivu chuktak.	"Pete already chopped them."
15.	Apo'ikne aniak.	"I helped *him*."
16.	Inepo aaniak.	"*I* helped him."
17.	Uka o'owtam vichak.	"They saw the man."
18.	Peo uka miisita temuk.	"Pete kicked the cat."
19.	U o'ow uka karita veetak.	"The man burned the house."
20.	Inepo apo'ik vichak.	"*I* saw *him*."
21.	U teeve o'ow maasoye'e.	"The tall man is deer-dancing."
22.	Peo teeve o'owta vichak.	"Pete saw a tall man."
23.	Inepo uka chukwi chuu'uta vichak.	"*I* saw the black dog."
24.	Inepo enchi aniak.	"*I* helped *you*."
25.	Vempo uka karita veetak.	"*They* burned the house."
26.	Uka vachita'e vichak.	"You saw the corn."
27.	Empo ye'ek, aapo into bʷiikak.	"*You* danced, and *he* sang."
28.	Tuuka'e aniak.	"You helped yesterday."

A. In the spaces provided, write the Yaqui morphemes corresponding to the English glosses on the right. (Yaqui has a full set of pronouns for all numbers and persons, but they are not all used in this exercise.)

1. Verbs

	Yaqui form	English gloss
a.	_____	"burned"
b.	_____	"chopped"
c.	_____	"danced"
d.	_____	"deer-dancing"
e.	_____	"grabbed"
f.	_____	"helped"
g.	_____	"kicked"
h.	_____	"left"
i.	_____	"saw"
j.	_____	"sold"
k.	_____	"sang"
l.	_____	"worked"

2. Full pronouns: Subject

	Yaqui form	English gloss
a.	_____	1st person (sg.)
b.	_____	2nd person (sg.)
c.	_____	3rd person (sg.)
d.	(not in data)	1st person (pl.)
e.	(not in data)	2nd person (pl.)
f.	_____	3rd person (pl.)

3. Full pronouns: Object

	Yaqui form	English gloss
a.	_____	1st person (sg.)
b.	_____	2nd person (sg.)
c.	_____	3rd person (sg.)

4. Clitic pronouns: Subject

	Yaqui form	English gloss
a.	_____	1st person (sg.)
b.	_____	2nd person (sg.)
c.	_____ (not in data) _____	3rd person (sg.)
d.	_____	1st person (pl.)
e.	_____ (not in data) _____	2nd person (pl.)
f.	_____	3rd person (pl.)

5. Clitic pronouns: Object

	Yaqui form	English gloss
a.	_____	3rd person (sg.)
b.	_____	3rd person (pl.)

6. Definite articles

	Yaqui form	English gloss
a.	_____	subject
b.	_____	object

B. The *perfective* form of a Yaqui verb is translated with the English past tense. What is the most likely part of each verb that carries the meaning "perfective"? (Two verbs in sentences 1–28 do not carry this morpheme. One is inherently perfective and the other is not perfective.)

C. How are grammatical relations marked in Yaqui? Use the following terms in your answer: *subject pronouns*, *object pronouns*, *independent pronouns*, *case-marking suffix*. (Hint: *-po*, which looks like it might be a case-marking suffix, is not.)

D. Based on the above data, which are representative of Yaqui as a whole, discuss the word order properties of Yaqui sentences.

4.15 Simple Sentences 5: Dyirbal

The following sentences are from Dyirbal, a language spoken in North Queensland, Australia. Study the sentences carefully, and answer the questions that follow.

Do not try to account for morphological changes in the verb "hit." Also, do not try to account for the phonetic differences between the case forms of nouns and pronouns.

The unfamiliar symbols in the Dyirbal sentences represent the following sounds: ḍ is a laminopalatal/alveolar stop; ɲ is an alveopalatal nasal; ṛ is a semiretroflex, r-like sound; and ŋ is a velar nasal.

1a. balan ḍugumbil balgan
 b. balgan balan ḍugumbil
     "Someone is hitting the woman."

2a. ŋayguna balgan
 b. balgan ŋayguna
     "Someone is hitting me."

3a. bayi yaṛa yanuli
 b. yanuli bayi yaṛa
     "The man has to go out."

4a. balan ḍugumbil baŋgul yaṛaŋgu balgan
 b. balgan balan ḍugumbil baŋgul yaṛaŋgu
 c. baŋgul yaṛaŋgu balgan balan ḍugumbil
 d. balan ḍugumbil balgan baŋgul yaṛaŋgu
 e. balgan baŋgul yaṛaŋgu balan ḍugumbil
 f. baŋgul yaṛaŋgu balan ḍugumbil balgan
     "The man is hitting the woman."

5. bayi yaṛa baŋgun ḍugumbiru balgan
    "The woman is hitting the man."

6a. ŋaḍa balgalŋaɲu
 b. balgalŋaɲu ŋaḍa
     "I am hitting someone."

7a. balan ḍugumbil badiɲu
 b. badiɲu balan ḍugumbil
     "The woman falls down."

8a. ŋaḍa ŋinuna balgan
  b. ŋinuna ŋaḍa balgan
  c. balgan ŋaḍa ŋinuna
  d. balgan ŋinuna ŋaḍa
  e. ŋaḍa balgan ŋinuna
  f. ŋinuna balgan ŋaḍa
  "I'm hitting you."

9. bayi yaṛa balgalŋuɲu
  "The man is hitting someone."

10. ŋinda ŋayguna balgan
  "You're hitting me."

11. ŋaḍa bayi yaṛa balgan
  "I'm hitting the man."

12. bayi yaṛa yanu
  "The man is going."

13. bayi bargan baŋgul yaṛaŋgu ḍurgaɲu
  "The man is spearing the wallaby."

14. ŋayguna baŋgul yaṛaŋgu balgan
  "The man is hitting me."

15. bayi yaṛa baniɲu
  "The man is coming."

16. balan ḍugumbil yanu
  "The woman is going."

17. balan ḍugumbil baniɲu
  "The woman is coming."

18. ŋinda baniɲu
  "You are coming."

19. ŋaḍa baniɲu
  "I am coming."

Questions

A. Begin your analysis by filling in the spaces below with the appropriate Dyirbal forms.

  1. Subject of transitive sentence

  Dyirbal form   English gloss

  a. _____   "the man"

  b. _____   "the woman"

2. Object of transitive sentence

       Dyirbal form   English gloss

   a. _____   "the man"

   b. _____   "the woman"

   c. _____   "the wallaby"

3. Subject of intransitive sentence

       Dyirbal form   English gloss

   a. _____   "the man"

   b. _____   "the woman"

B. English and almost all European languages are classified as "nominative/accusative." In a nominative/accusative language the subject of a transitive sentence is marked in the same way as the subject of an intransitive sentence, but the object of a transitive sentence is marked differently. In English this difference shows up in the pronominal system. For example, *she* (the nominative form of the third person singular feminine pronoun) is used as the subject of both transitive and intransitive sentences; *her* (the object or accusative form of the third person singular feminine pronoun) is used in object position. Thus, *She hit the ball*, *She ran*, but *The fans watched her*.

In contrast, some of the world's languages—among them Dyirbal—are classified as "ergative/absolutive" languages. What property of the Dyirbal example sentences distinguishes Dyirbal from nominative/accusative languages? In other words, what property defines an ergative/absolutive language as opposed to a nominative/accusative language? Limit yourself to the words displayed in question A.

C. Although Dyirbal is classified as an ergative/absolutive language, it is more precisely defined as a "split ergative" language. To learn what a split ergative language is, begin by filling in the spaces below.

1. Subject of transitive sentence

   Dyirbal form   English gloss

   a. _____   "I"

   b. _____   "you"

2. Object of transitive sentence

   Dyirbal form   English gloss

   a. _____   "me"

   b. _____   "you"

3. Subject of intransitive sentence

   Dyirbal form   English gloss

   a. _____   "I"

   b. _____   "you"

Noting the contrast between the first and second person pronouns in questions C-1 through C-3 and the nouns in questions A-1 through A-3, state what you think the properties of a split ergative language are.

D. The variations in word order shown in example sentences 1–8 are also possible in the remaining sentences 9–19. Discuss the role of word order in Dyirbal sentences. For example, does word order play a role in determining grammatical relations (subject, object, etc.) in Dyirbal?

4.16 Simple Sentences 6: Japanese

Examine the Japanese sentences 1–7 and answer the questions that follow.

Assume that the particles *-ga*, *-o*, and *-ni* indicate whether the noun phrase to which they are attached is functioning as subject, object, or indirect object, respectively.

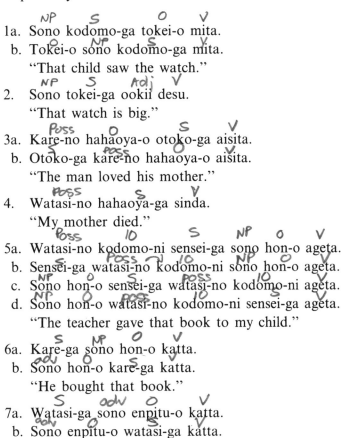

1a. Sono kodomo-ga tokei-o mita.
 b. Tokei-o sono kodomo-ga mita.
  "That child saw the watch."

2. Sono tokei-ga ookii desu.
  "That watch is big."

3a. Kare-no hahaoya-o otoko-ga aisita.
 b. Otoko-ga kare-no hahaoya-o aisita.
  "The man loved his mother."

4. Watasi-no hahaoya-ga sinda.
  "My mother died."

5a. Watasi-no kodomo-ni sensei-ga sono hon-o ageta.
 b. Sensei-ga watasi-no kodomo-ni sono hon-o ageta.
 c. Sono hon-o sensei-ga watasi-no kodomo-ni ageta.
 d. Sono hon-o watasi-no kodomo-ni sensei-ga ageta.
  "The teacher gave that book to my child."

6a. Kare-ga sono hon-o katta.
 b. Sono hon-o kare-ga katta.
  "He bought that book."

7a. Watasi-ga sono enpitu-o katta.
 b. Sono enpitu-o watasi-ga katta.
  "I bought that pencil."

A. Provide the Japanese equivalents to the English words below.

Japanese form   English gloss

1. _____ "child"

2. _____ "watch"

3. _____ "man"

4. _____ "mother"

5. _____ "book"

6. _____ "I"

7. _____ "pencil"

8. _____ "saw"

9. _____ "is"

10. _____ "loved"

11. _____ "that"

12. _____ "big"

13. _____ "he"

14. _____ "died"

B. How is the possessive formed in Japanese? (Examine sentences 3, 4, and 5.)

Adding "-no" to a pronoun or noun.

C. How would you translate *that man's child* into Japanese?

Sono otoko-no kodomo

D. What constraints do there appear to be on word order in Japanese? (Be sure to examine all the variations on word order in sentences 1–7 before answering this question. You will find some elements whose order never varies.)

all verbs are last
adverbs ~~before~~ immediately before noun they modify
poss "

E. What is the Japanese sentence for *That mother's child gave the watch to that child*?

Sono hahaoya-no kodomo-ga tokei-o sono kodomo-ni ageta.

4.17 Complex Sentences: Japanese

In the following examples from Japanese, the a-sentences are simple sentences and each b-sentence contains a relative clause based on the corresponding a-sentence. Examine the sentences and answer questions A–E.

When -*wa* appears, it marks the subject of the verb of the main clause of the sentence; otherwise, the subject is marked with -*ga*. Furthermore, assume that -*o* indicates direct object.

1a. Kinoo John-ga otoko-o nagutta.
  "Yesterday, John hit a man."
 b. Watasi-wa kinoo John-ga nagutta otoko-o mita.
  "I saw the man whom John hit yesterday."

2a. Kinoo John-ga otoko-o nagutta.
  "Yesterday, John hit a man."
 b. Kinoo John-ga nagutta otoko-ga paatii-ni kita.
  "The man whom John hit yesterday came to the party."

3a. Kinoo otoko-ga John-o nagutta.
  "Yesterday, a man hit John."
 b. Watasi-wa kinoo John-o nagutta otoko-o mita.
  "I saw the man who hit John yesterday."

4a. Watasi-wa Hanako-kara hon-o karita.
  "I borrowed a book from Hanako."
 b. Otooto-wa watasi-ga Hanako-kara karita hon-o nakusita.
  "My brother lost the book which I borrowed from Hanako."

5a. Watasi-wa Hanako-kara hon-o karita.
  "I borrowed a book from Hanako."
 b. Watasi-ga Hanako-kara karita hon-wa totemo omosiroi.
  "The book which I borrowed from Hanako is very interesting."

Questions

A. Provide the Japanese equivalents for the English words and phrases below.

	Japanese form	English gloss
1.	_____	"hit"
2.	_____	"I"
3.	_____	"is interesting"
4.	_____	"came"
5.	_____	"book"
6.	_____	"man"
7.	_____	"very"
8.	_____	"to"
9.	_____	"lost"
10.	_____	"saw"
11.	_____	"party"
12.	_____	"yesterday"
13.	_____	"borrowed"
14.	_____	"(my) brother"
15.	_____	"from"

B. In English, a relative clause may be introduced by a relative pronoun such as *who* or *which* (*the book which you borrowed*). Does Japanese have such a word that indicates the presence of a relative clause?

C. In the noun phrase *the child who cried a lot, the child* is called the "head" of the relative clause. In English, the "head" occurs to the left of the relative clause. Where does the "head" of the relative clause occur in a Japanese noun phrase?

D. For each of the b-sentences, draw brackets around the noun phrase that contains the relative clause. Be sure to put the relative clause within the brackets for the noun phrase in the following manner:

1b. Watasi -wa [_{NP} kinoo John -ga nagutta otoko _{NP}] -o mita.

"I saw the man whom John hit yesterday."

2b. Kinoo John -ga nagutta otoko -ga paatii -ni kita.

"The man whom John hit yesterday came to the party."

3b. Watasi -wa kinoo John -o nagutta otoko -o mita.

"I saw the man who hit John yesterday."

4b. Otooto -wa watasi -ga Hanako -kara karita hon -o nakusita.

"My brother lost the book which I borrowed from Hanako."

5b. Watasi -ga Hanako -kara karita hon -wa totemo omosiroi.

"The book which I borrowed from Hanako is very interesting."

E. Translate the noun phrase *the book which (my) brother lost* into Japanese.

4.18 Morphosyntax 1: Telugu

Each of the following words in Telugu (a Dravidian language spoken in India) is translated into English by an entire sentence. Each word is complex, that is, composed of several morphemes. Analyze the words by identifying the morphemes occurring in each word, and answer questions A–C.

The phonetic values of the symbols used can be determined from the chart in appendix 3. An exact understanding of the value of the phonetic symbols is not necessary to carry out the analysis required for this exercise. For example, the *d* with a dot under it (*ḍ*) can be understood simply as a "different kind of *d*" that appears in Telugu but not in English.

The verbal morphology of Telugu is very complex, a fact that is not reflected in this exercise.

	Telugu form	English gloss
1.	ceppɛɛnu	"I told"
2.	ceppincunu	"I cause (someone) to tell"
3.	cuustaam	"We will see"
4.	ceppɛɛm	"We told"
5.	ceppanu	"I will not tell"
6.	navvincum	"We cause (someone) to laugh"
7.	cuustunnaaḍu	"He is seeing"
8.	ceppɛɛyi	"They told"
9.	koḍataanu	"I will beat"
10.	paaḍataanu	"I will sing"
11.	ceppɛɛru	"You (pl.) told"
12.	ceppavu	"You (sg.) will not tell"
13.	ceppɛɛvu	"You (sg.) told"
14.	ceppam	"We will not tell"
15.	ceppɛɛḍu	"He told"
16.	cuusɛɛḍu	"He saw"
17.	cepparu	"You (pl.) will not tell"
18.	koḍatunnaayi	"They are beating"
19.	ceestunnaanu	"I am doing"
20.	aḍugutaam	"We will ask"
21.	ceesɛɛnu	"I did"
22.	aḍugutaaḍu	"He will ask"

Questions

A. In the spaces below, list the Telugu morphemes that correspond to the English words on the right.

1. Verbs

	Telugu morpheme	English gloss
a.	_____	"tell"
b.	_____	"sing"
c.	_____	"see"
d.	_____	"laugh"
e.	_____	"ask"
f.	_____	"beat"
g.	_____	"do"

2. Person marking of subjects

	Telugu morpheme	English gloss
a.	_____	"I"
b.	_____	"you (sg.)"
c.	_____	"he"
d.	_____	"we"
e.	_____	"you (pl.)"
f.	_____	"they"

3. Others

	Telugu morpheme	English gloss
a.	_____	past tense
b.	_____	present tense (-*ing* form in English gloss)
c.	_____	future tense
d.	_____	negative future tense
e.	_____	causative

B. List the order in which the morphemes occur in the Telugu words. (For example, in *ceppɛɛnu*, which morpheme comes first? The verb? The subject? Tense?) Use terms such as *causative*, *tense*, *subject*, *verb*.

C. Translate the following English sentences into Telugu.

1. You (pl.) are singing. _____

2. They will not laugh. _____

3. You (sg.) will cause (someone) to ask. _____

4.19 Morphosyntax 2: Swahili

As was true of the Telugu words in exercise 4.18, each of the following words in Swahili (a language of the Niger-Congo family spoken in Africa) is translated into English by an entire sentence. Each word is complex, that is, composed of several morphemes. Analyze the forms by identifying the morphemes occurring in each word, and answer the questions that follow.

	Swahili form	English gloss
1.	aliwaandika	"He/she wrote you (pl.)"
2.	ninakujua	"I know you (sg.)"
3.	anasoma	"He/she reads"
4.	ulituuliza	"You (sg.) asked us"
5.	tulikuona	"We saw you (sg.)"
6.	anamjua	"He/she knows him/her"
7.	mtasoma	"You (pl.) will read"
8.	walimpiga	"They hit him/her" (past)
9.	umeandika	"You (sg.) have just written"
10.	mlimpiga	"You (pl.) hit him/her" (past)
11.	anakujua	"He/she knows you (sg.)"
12.	mtaniona	"You (pl.) will see me"
13.	nimembusu	"I have just kissed him/her"
14.	walisoma	"They read" (past)
15.	nitawabusu	"I will kiss you (pl.)"
16.	tumewaandika	"We have just written you (pl.)"
17.	utanibusu	"You (sg.) will kiss me"
18.	utatupiga	"You (sg.) will hit us"
19.	wamewauliza	"They have just asked them"
20.	tumewauliza	"We have just asked them"

A. In the spaces below, list the Swahili morphemes that correspond to the English words on the right.

1. Subjects

   Swahili morpheme   English gloss

   a. _____   "I"

   b. _____   "you (sg.)"

   c. _____   "he/she"

   d. _____   "we"

   e. _____   "you (pl.)"

   f. _____   "they"

2. Objects

   Swahili morpheme   English gloss

   a. _____   "me"

   b. _____   "you (sg.)"

   c. _____   "him/her"

   d. _____   "us"

   e. _____   "you (pl.)"

   f. _____   "them"

3. "Tenses"

   Swahili morpheme   English gloss

   a. _____   present

   b. _____   future

   c. _____   past

   d. _____   recent perfective ("have just *X*'d")

4. Verbs

Swahili morpheme	English gloss
a. _____	"write"
b. _____	"ask"
c. _____	"read"
d. _____	"see"
e. _____	"know"
f. _____	"hit"
g. _____	"kiss"

B. List the order in which morphemes occur in the Swahili words given in examples 1–20. Use terms such as *verb*, *subject*, and *object*.

C. *Bonus.* The morphemes for second person plural subjects and third person singular objects involve a certain phonological complication: as examples 21–25 show, each morpheme appears in two different forms, and the shape that occurs in a particular word can be predicted from the phonological environment (the surrounding sounds) in which the morpheme appears.

The forms in 24 and 25 contain another present tense marker, -a-, which indicates that the action of the verb either is an established state or is generally the case. The English present tense is very close in meaning to the Swahili tense marked with -a-.

21. nilimwandika   "I wrote him/her"
22. tulimwona   "We saw him/her"
23. unamwuliza   "You (sg.) ask him/her"
24. mwamwandika   "You (pl.) write him/her"
25. mwasoma   "You (pl.) read"

Considering examples 21–25 and referring back to examples 1–20, describe the environment that conditions the appearance of each of the two forms in the most general statement you can devise.

Name Jeremy Garber

Section

4.20 Morphosyntax 3: Classical Nahuatl (Aztec)

Isolate the morphemes for the following forms of Classical Nahuatl (a Uto-Aztecan language spoken in Mexico) and answer questions A–D.

This exercise introduces a new feature. Sometimes in a language, as in Nahuatl, the lack of an overt morpheme has meaning. Some of the examples in 1–21, then, will have an element of meaning for which no phonetically realized morpheme is present. Represent these phonetically empty morphemes in the appropriate spaces below with $\emptyset$ (the symbol used by linguists to indicate such morphemes).

This exercise uses an alphabet somewhat different from the one Nahuatl speakers use to write the modern language. The current Nahuatl alphabet is based on the conventions used to write Spanish. In this exercise (as in the current Nahuatl alphabet) the letters *ch* correspond to the sound represented by *ch* in English, as in the word *chip* (see *Linguistics*, p. 70). A colon following a vowel indicates that the vowel is long.

	Nahuatl form	English gloss
1.	nicho:ka	"I cry"
2.	nicho:kahi	"I am crying"
3.	ankochihih	"You (pl.) are sleeping"
4.	tikochih	"We sleep"
5.	kochiya	"He was sleeping"
6.	kwi:kas	"He will sing"
7.	ankochiyah	"You (pl.) were sleeping"
8.	nicho:kas	"I will cry"
9.	cho:kayah	"They were crying"
10.	tikochi	"You (sg.) sleep"
11.	ancho:kah	"You (pl.) cry"
12.	tikochis	"You (sg.) will sleep"
13.	ticho:kayah	"We were crying"
14.	cho:ka	"He cries"
15.	kochini	"He is sleeping"
16.	ancho:kayah	"You (pl.) were crying"
17.	ticho:kanih	"We are crying"
18.	kwi:kah	"They sing"
19.	tikwi:kani	"You (sg.) are singing"
20.	nikwi:kaya	"I was singing"
21.	cho:kanih	"They are crying"

Questions

A. In the spaces below, list the Classical Nahuatl morphemes that correspond to the English words on the right.

1. Verbs

Nahuatl morpheme	English gloss
a. _kochi_	"sleep"
b. _kwi:ka_	"sing"
c. _cho:ka_	"cry"

2. Person marking

Nahuatl morpheme	English gloss
a. _ni-_	"I"
b. _ti-_	"you (sg.)"
c. _Ø_	"he"
d. _ti-_ _-h_	"we"
e. _an-_ _-h_	"you (pl.)"
f. _-h_	"they"

3. Tense marking

Nahuatl morpheme	English gloss
a. _Ø_	present
b. _-ni_	customary present (corresponds in English to the present progressive—that is, -*ing* forms)
c. _-ya_	imperfect (translated in English as a past progressive—that is, "was V-ing," where V stands for any verb)
d. _-s_	future

B. Give the order of the morphemes in Nahuatl, using the category labels found in question A (*verb*, *subject*, *tense*, etc.).

subject   verb tense pluralization

C. Translate the following Nahuatl forms into English.

1. tikwi:ka   you (sg.) sing

2. cho:kani   he is crying

3. nikochiya   I was sleeping

D. Translate the following English sentences into Nahuatl.

1. You (sg.) are sleeping.   tikochini

2. They will sing.   kwi:kash

3. We cry.   ticho:kah

Name _____

Section _____

4.21 Morphosyntax 4: Merkin

Analyze the following sentences and answer the questions that follow. In this language, the words on the left correspond to the English sentences on the right. Compare the properties of Merkin with those of Telugu and Swahili (exercises 4.18 and 4.19). For symbols that may be unfamiliar to you, refer to appendix 3 or to chapter 3 in *Linguistics*.

	Merkin form	English gloss
1.	alhɪdəm	"I will hit him/them"
2.	šɪlsiy	"She will see"
3.	wɪlteykɪt	"We will take it"
4.	hiydhɪdəm	"He would hit him/them"
5.	yuwsiyəm	"You see him/them"
6.	alsiyər	"I will see her"
7.	alsiyɪt	"I will see it"
8.	šiydsiyəm	"She would see him/them"
9.	ðɛlnowəm	"They will know him/them"
10.	wɪlnowɨt	"We will know it"
11.	ɪdɨdteykɨt	"It would take it"
12.	ðeydlʌvər	"They would love her"
13.	hiydlʌvəm	"He would love him/them"
14.	hɪlnowər	"He will know her"
15.	aydlʌvɨt	"I would love it"
16.	ɪdɨdteykər	"It would take her"
17.	yʊlhɪdəm	"You will hit him/them"
18.	hiydnowəm	"He would know him/them"
19.	wiydteykɨt	"We would take it"
20.	ðɛlnowəm	"They will know him/them"
21.	yuwdhɪdər	"You would hit her"
22.	ɪdəlsiyər	"It will see her"

Questions

A. In the spaces below, list the Merkin morphemes that correspond to the English translations.

   1. Verbs

      Merkin morpheme   English gloss

     a. _____   "hit"

     b. _____   "love"

     c. _____   "know"

     d. _____   "take"

     e. _____   "see"

   2. Subject marking

      Merkin morpheme   English gloss

     a. _____   1st person singular

        _____

     b. _____   2nd person singular

        _____

     c. _____   3rd person singular masculine

        _____

     d. _____   3rd person singular feminine

        _____

     e. _____   3rd person singular inanimate

     f. _____   1st person plural

        _____

     g. _____   3rd person plural

        _____

3. Object marking

Merkin morpheme	English gloss
a. _____	3rd person singular masculine
b. _____	3rd person singular feminine
c. _____	3rd person singular inanimate
d. _____	3rd person plural

4. Modality marking

Merkin morpheme	English gloss
a. _____	future
_____	
b. _____	conditional
_____	

B. What is the word order in a Merkin sentence? Use terms such as *subject*, *object*, *verb*.

C. The subject-marking morphemes occur in both a long and a short form. What is the conditioning environment for each form?

D. The modality morphemes occur in both a long and a short form. What is the conditioning environment for each form?

4.22 Special Topic 1: C-Command

Consider the following tree and answer questions A–F:

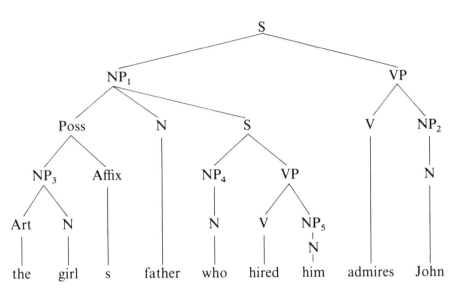

Assume the following definition of c(onstituent)-command (see also *Linguistics*, p. 200):

Node A c-commands node B if and only if the first branching node that dominates A also dominates B (condition: A does not dominate B and vice versa).

Questions

A. Does NP$_1$ c-command NP$_2$? Why or why not?

B. Does NP$_2$ c-command NP$_1$? Why or why not?

C. Does NP$_1$ c-command NP$_3$? Why or why not?

D. Does NP$_5$ c-command NP$_2$? Why or why not?

E. Assume that *him* and *John* can be used to refer to the same individual in the sentence *The girl's father who hired him admires John*. Does *John* have to c-command the pronoun *him* in order to be coreferential with it? Explain.

F. Provide another example sentence where a pronoun occurs before a noun phrase, such as *John*, and is coreferential with it.

4.23 Special Topic 2: Reflexive (English)

The following quotation is taken from an English grammar book:

Limitations on Active-Passive Conversions:
You should be aware that not all actives with direct objects can be converted into passives. Actives in which the direct object is a reflexive do not convert successfully. "He hated himself" converts into the unacceptable *"Himself was hated by him." (Cook and Suter 1980, 75)

If the unacceptability of *Himself was hated by him is accounted for by saying that an active cannot be converted into a passive when the direct object is a reflexive, then sentences like those given below would presumably involve a different kind of oddity since they are *not* active-passive pairs.

1a. John loves himself.
 b. Himself loves John.   (odd)

2a. Mary looked at herself in the mirror.
 b. Herself looked at Mary in the mirror.   (odd)

3a. The bosses paid themselves adequately.
 b. Themselves paid the bosses adequately.   (odd)

4a. Mary forced John to wash himself.
 b. Mary forced himself to wash John.   (odd with *John = himself*)

5a. Mary expected John to wash himself.
 b. Mary expected himself to wash John.   (odd with *himself = John*)

However, the odd b-sentences and the passive sentence *Himself was hated by him* do in fact have something in common. Study these sentences and answer questions A–C.

Questions

A. What do the b-sentences of 1–5 and the passive sentence *Himself was hated by him* have in common?

B. Check your answer to question A against the data below. What revisions are necessary in order to account for the new data? (Review *Linguistics*, pp. 192–195 and 199–201.)

6a. The man believes that himself will win.   (odd)
 b. The man believes that he will win.

7a. The man loves the woman who admires himself.   (odd)
 b. The man loves the woman who admires him.

8a. That the boy likes herself pleased the girl.   (odd)
 b. That the boy likes her pleased the girl.

9a. The boy knows that himself told the truth.   (odd)
 b. The boy knows that he told the truth.

10a. The girl who saw himself knows the man.   (odd)
 b. The girl who saw him knows the man.

C. An account of the unacceptability of *Himself was hated by him* that is based on the assumption that an active cannot be converted into a passive when the direct object is a reflexive misses something important. Provide a more general account for the oddity of the b-sentences in 1–5 and the a-sentences in 6–10 that subsumes the passive example. (Hint: Review exercise 4.22.)

4.24 Special Topic 3: Reflexive (Russian)

Study the Russian sentences in lists I and II and answer the questions that follow.
For the purposes of the exercise, ignore the prefix on the verb in sentence 6.
The prepositions used in this exercise are *ot* "from," *k* "for," *pod* "under," and *v* "in."

List I	List II
1. Ya ukryl detei ot solntsa.	Ya ukrylsya ot solntsa.
"I hid the children from the sun."	"I hid myself from the sun."
2. On gotovil detei k ekzamenu.	On gotovilsya k ekzamenu.
"He prepared the children for the exam."	"He prepared himself for the exam."
3. On videl detei pod stolom.	On videlsya v zerkalo.
"He saw the children under the table."	"He saw himself in the mirror."
4. On kupal detei.	On kupalsya.
"He bathed the children."	"He bathed himself."
5. On odeval detei.	On odevalsya.
"He dressed the children."	"He dressed himself."
6. On rezal xleb.	On porezalsya.
"He cut the bread."	"He cut himself."
7. On prichesal detei.	On prichesalsya.
"He combed the children."	"He combed himself (his hair)."
8. On xotel ubit' zayatsa.	On xotel ubitsya.
"He wanted to kill a rabbit."	"He wanted to kill himself."

Questions

A. Write the Russian words corresponding to the English glosses.

	Russian form	English gloss
1.	_____	"table"
2.	_____	"I"
3.	_____	"he"

4. _____ "sun"

5. _____ "children"

6. _____ "exam"

7. _____ "bread"

8. _____ "mirror"

9. _____ "rabbit"

B. The verbs (except for *xotel*) appear in two forms. For each verb listed below, provide the two forms.

Shorter form   Longer form

1. _____ _____ "hid"

2. _____ _____ "prepared"

3. _____ _____ "saw"

4. _____ _____ "bathed"

5. _____ _____ "dressed"

6. _____ _____ "cut"

7. _____ _____ "combed"

8. _____ _____ "kill"

C. When does the longer form of the verb occur? That is, state the conditioning environment for the longer form of the verb.

D. When does the shorter form of the verb occur? Under what conditions?

4.25 Special Topic 4: Reflexive (Japanese)

Study the sentences in lists I and II and answer the questions that follow.

Assume that the particles -*wa*, -*o*, and -*ni* mark subject, object, and indirect object, respectively. (Note: *Taroo* is a man's name and *Mieko* is a woman's name.)

List I

1a. Taroo-wa Mieko-o sinraisiteiru.
 b. Mieko-o Taroo-wa sinraisiteiru.
 "Taro trusts Mieko."

2a. Taroo-wa Mieko-o hihansita.
 b. Mieko-o Taroo-wa hihansita.
 "Taro criticized Mieko."

3a. Taroo-wa Mieko-o sensei-ni
 urikonda.
 b. Mieko-o Taroo-wa sensei-ni
 urikonda.
 "Taro presented Mieko to the
 teacher."

4a. Mieko-wa Taroo-o aisiteiru.
 b. Taroo-o Mieko-wa aisiteiru.
 "Mieko loves Taro."

5a. Mieko-wa Taroo-o keibetsusiteiru.
 b. Taroo-o Mieko-wa keibetsusiteiru.
 "Mieko despises Taro."

6a. Taroo-wa Mieko-o tataita.
 b. Mieko-o Taroo-wa tataita.
 "Taro hit Mieko."

List II

1a. Taroo-wa zibun-o sinraisiteiru.
 b. Zibun-o Taroo-wa sinraisiteiru.
 "Taro trusts himself."

2a. Taroo-wa zibun-o hihansita.
 b. Zibun-o Taroo-wa hihansita.
 "Taro criticized himself."

3a. Taroo-wa zibun-o sensei-ni
 urikonda.
 b. Zibun-o Taroo-wa sensei-ni
 urikonda.
 "Taro presented himself to the
 teacher."

4a. Mieko-wa zibun-o aisiteiru.
 b. Zibun-o Mieko-wa aisiteiru.
 "Mieko loves herself."

5a. Mieko-wa zibun-o keibetsusiteiru.
 b. Zibun-o Mieko-wa keibetsusiteiru.
 "Mieko despises herself."

6a. Taroo-wa zibun-o tataita.
 b. Zibun-o Taroo-wa tataita.
 "Taro hit himself."

Questions

A. Provide the Japanese equivalents to the English words below by filling in the blanks.

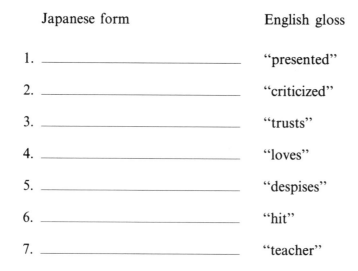

Japanese form   English gloss

1. _____   "presented"

2. _____   "criticized"

3. _____   "trusts"

4. _____   "loves"

5. _____   "despises"

6. _____   "hit"

7. _____   "teacher"

B. The word *zibun* translates into English as the reflexive *himself/herself*. Given the data in 1–6, what differences do you find between the English reflexive and *zibun*? (Hint: Compare where the "reflexive" words occur, their morphological form, and so forth.) In answering this question, you may find it useful to consult the previous exercises on reflexives.

4.26 Special Topic 5: Reflexive (Japanese)

In this exercise you will be exploring the use of the Japanese reflexive *zibun* in embedded (subordinate) clauses. Examine sentences 1–3 and answer the questions that follow.

In these examples the particle *-wa* marks the subject of the verb of the main clause of the sentence, and *-ga* marks the subject of the embedded clause.

1a. Taroo-wa Hanako-ga zibun-o aisiteiru to omotteimasu.
   "Taro thinks that Hanako loves herself."   *or*
   "Taro thinks that Hanako loves him (Taro)."
 b. Taroo-wa zibun-ga Hanako-o aisiteiru to omotteimasu.
   "Taro thinks that he (Taro) loves Hanako."

2a. Taroo-wa Hanako-ga zibun-o mita to itta.
   "Taro said that Hanako saw herself."   *or*
   "Taro said that Hanako saw him (Taro)."
 b. Taroo-wa zibun-ga Hanako-o mita to itta.
   "Taro said that he (Taro) saw Hanako."

3a. Taroo-wa Hanako-ga zibun-o hihansita to sinziteiru.
   "Taro believes that Hanako criticized herself."   *or*
   "Taro believes that Hanako criticized him (Taro)."
 b. Taroo-wa zibun-ga Hanako-o hihansita to sinziteiru.
   "Taro believes that he (Taro) criticized Hanako."

Questions

A. Provide the Japanese equivalents to the English words below by filling in the blanks.

Japanese form	English gloss
1. _____	"thinks"
2. _____	"believes"
3. _____	"said"
4. _____	"that"

B. Sentences 1a, 2a, and 3a all have two interpretations with respect to *zibun*. What is the difference between these two interpretations? Pay close attention to the English translations that have been provided.

C. None of the b-sentences are ambiguous in the way the a-sentences are. What is the syntactic difference between the two sets of sentences that accounts for the fact that the b-sentences have only one interpretation, whereas the a-sentences have two?

D. Review exercise 4.23 on the English reflexive, especially question B. Compare and contrast Japanese *zibun* with English *himself/herself*. Consider the restrictions on the relative positions of the "antecedent" (*Taroo* in example 6 of exercise 4.25) and the "anaphor" (*zibun* and *himself/herself*) as well as any special restrictions one language might have on the "antecedent" with regard to grammatical relations.

5 Semantics

5.1 Compositional and Noncompositional Meanings

The cartoon accompanying each of the following expressions depicts its compositional meaning—that is, the meaning determined by putting together the meanings of its parts. However, each expression also has a noncompositional (idiomatic) meaning. Consider the expressions and the compositional meanings depicted by the cartoons; you will be asked to supply their noncompositional meanings.

1. He's sitting on the fence.

2. They put the cart before the horse.

3. He's barking up the wrong tree.

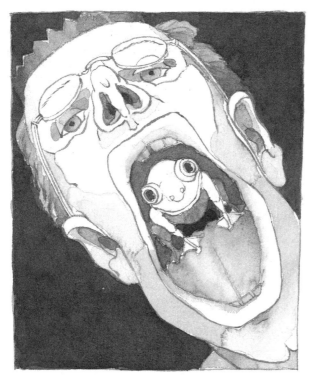

4. He's got a frog in his throat.

Question

State the noncompositional (idiomatic) meaning for expressions 1–4.

1.

2.

3.

4.

5.2 Ambiguous Words

Questions

A. The following words are ambiguous. Some have two meanings; others have more. For each word, define or give a synonym for two meanings. Use your intuitions (not the dictionary).

1. charge

   a. *galloping cavalry advancement*

   b. *transfer debt onto a credit card*

2. claim

   a. *say something is yours*

   b. *say something is true*

3. park

   a. *stop the car (verb)*

   b. *a landscaped area (noun)*

4. soil

   a. *get something dirty (v)*

   b. *earth; dirt (N)*

5. heat

   a. *make something warmer (v)*

   b. *the sensation of increased molecular activity (n)*

185

B. Provide five examples of words that are ambiguous. Give two different meanings for each one.

1. _throw_

    a. the act of propelling something

    b. a small blanket

2. _rock_

    a. move ryhthymically back & forth

    b. a hard mineral

3. _plant_

    a. ~~Condition~~ a vegetable

    b. to put seeds in the ground

4. _____

    a.

    b.

5. _____

    a.

    b.

5.3 Ambiguous Sentences

Question

The following sentences are ambiguous. Provide a paraphrase for each reading or interpretation.

1. The new computer and printer were left at the door.

   a.

   b.

2. The chicken is ready to eat.

   a. *The chicken wants to eat something.*

   b. *We can now eat the fully cooked chicken.*

3. Ringing bells did not annoy him.

   a. *Bells that rang ~~did not annoy bells~~ did not annoy him.*

   b. *The act of bell-ringing did not annoy him.*

4. He likes galloping horses.

   a.

   b.

5.4 Homophony and Polysemy

Homophonous words have identical pronunciations but different, not obviously related meanings: *bank* "side of a river" versus *bank* "financial institution." In contrast, a *polysemous word* is a single word that has several closely related meanings: *heart* "(1) organ that supplies blood to the circulatory system; (2) innermost area."

Question

Indicate whether each word below is an instance of homophony or polysemy. Defend your answer in each case by discussing the meanings of the word(s). If the relation is one of polysemy, discuss in what ways the various meanings can be related.

1. accommodation (lodging; anything that meets a need)

    polysemy

2. nail (fingernail or toenail; carpenter's nail)

    homophony

3. admission (confession; entrance fee)

    homophony polysemy

4. plane (aircraft; flat or level surface)

homophony   (polysemy?)

5. fire (*as in* forest fire; cause someone to become unemployed)

homophony

5.5 Evaluative and Emotive Meaning

A word may be associated with more than its literal meaning; it may have emotional connotations as well. Bertrand Russell once offered the following paradigm to illustrate this distinction:

I am firm.
You are obstinate.
He is a pig-headed fool.

The same person might be correctly described by all three terms, but their emotional effects are quite different.

Questions

A. The following triples are further examples of "emotive conjugations." In each case, first state the literal meaning shared by the words and then discuss how they differ in terms of expressed evaluation and emotional impact. Choose five of the following examples to discuss.

  1. tavern, bar, dive

A place where alcohol is served. "A tavern" implies elegance, and usually shared

  2. fairer sex, female, broad

3. resign, quit, throw in the towel

4. release, discharge, fire (from a job)

5. meticulous, fussy, nit-picking

6. car, jalopy, heap

7. between jobs, out of work, on the dole

8. separate from, walk out on, desert

9. discriminating, exclusive, snobbish

10. nonsense, baloney, a crock

11. father, dad, old man

B. Provide three more sets of examples of "emotive conjugations."

1. film, movie, flick

2. erotica, pornography, smut

3. mental illness, insanity, craziness

5.6 Special Topic 1: Idioms and Pronouns

Examine sentences 1–12 and answer the questions that follow.

For the purposes of this exercise, consider only the idiomatic interpretation of each sentence. You will find that—considered in this light—all the b-sentences are odd. For example, it is odd to say *That lady is beating his head against a brick wall* under the idiomatic interpretation that the lady is trying to do something impossible.

1a. John lost his head.
 b. They lost his head.   (odd)

2a. She is out of her mind.
 b. The man over there is out of their minds.   (odd)

3a. Bob is off his rocker.
 b. You are off his rocker.   (odd)

4a. I gnashed my teeth.
 b. We gnashed my teeth.   (odd)

5a. You craned your neck.
 b. He craned your neck.   (odd)

6a. She's flipped her wig.
 b. Bob's flipped my wig.   (odd)

7a. The child stuck out her tongue.
 b. The girl stuck out his tongue.   (odd)

8a. I broke my head over that problem.
 b. I broke your head over that problem.   (odd)

9a. The man is beating his head against a brick wall.
 b. That lady is beating his head against a brick wall.   (odd)

10a. You should bite your tongue.
 b. He should bite your tongue.   (odd)

11a. That poor woman is pulling her hair out.
 b. That poor man is pulling her hair out.   (odd)

12a. My mother is always wringing her hands.
 b. My father is always wringing her hands.   (odd)

A. What property do all the a-sentences have that is not shared by the b-sentences? In particular, look at the subject of the sentence and the possessive pronoun (*his, her, your*).

B. How would you account for the oddity of the b-sentences? That is, why is it odd to say something like *He broke my head over that problem*?

Name

Section

5.7 Special Topic 2: Ambiguity and Quantifiers

Question

Exercises 5.2 and 5.3 involve lexical and (surface) syntactic ambiguity, respectively. The cooccurrence of quantifier phrases (*every student*, *somebody*, *anybody*, etc.) with pronouns (*he*, *she*, etc.) often gives rise to ambiguity as well. For example, *Everyone likes her mother* means everyone likes her own mother or everyone likes, say, Mary's mother. For each sentence below, provide a paraphrase for each reading or interpretation. (These examples have been selected from the following works: Reinhart 1983, Wasow 1979, Postal 1971, Hornstein 1984.)

1. I talked with every student about his problems.

    a.

    b.

2. In his drawer each of the managers keeps a gun.

    a.

    b.

3. Someone liked his proposal about garbage removal.

    a.

    b.

4. Nobody would keep matches near his child's crib.

    a.

    b.

5. Everyone believes that a pretty woman loves him.

   a.

   b.

6. Each of Mary's sons hated his brothers.

   a.

   b.

5.8 Special Topic 3: Grammaticalization of Semantic Properties

Semantic features or categories that are overtly expressed in the grammar of a language are said to be *grammaticalized*. One example involves plurality. The semantic feature of plurality is grammaticalized in European languages: it appears as a morphological affix on the noun (e.g., the English plural {s, z, iz}). In contrast, Asian languages (e.g., Japanese and Chinese) do not have a morphological means to mark plurality. Another example involves the semantic feature of gender. English has lost most of its gender marking, but overt expression of this feature is still part of German, Swedish, French, and Spanish.

The semantic feature of physical shape is grammaticalized in a few Navajo verb roots. A speaker who wants to talk about "giving" or "holding" something in Navajo must choose a verb that indicates the physical properties of the given or held object. A few of the three dozen or so roots for Navajo handling verbs are given below.

	Navajo form	English gloss
1.	yish'aah	"I'm handling one round or bulky object"
2.	yishyį'	"I'm handling one bulky object"
3.	yishjaa'	"I'm handling granular plural objects"
4.	yishjool	"I'm handling noncompact matter (wool, hair, etc.)"
5.	yishką́	"I'm handling something in a vessel"
6.	yishlá	"I'm handling a slender, flexible object"
7.	yishtį́įh	"I'm handling a slender, stiff object"
8.	yishtsóós	"I'm handling a flexible, flat object"

In its system of classifiers, Chinese also grammaticalizes physical properties of objects. Some examples of the dozens of these classifiers that appear before nouns are given below. (The diacritics on the morphemes are tone markers.)

	Chinese form	English gloss
1.	yī běn N	"one (classifier) N" (used with books, notebooks)
2.	yī zhāng N	"one (classifier) N" (used with flat, sheetlike objects)
3.	yī gen N	"one (classifier) N" (used with long, slender objects)
4.	yī kè N	"one (classifier) N" (used with plants)
5.	yī kuài N	"one (classifier) N" (used with pieces or lumps of an object)
6.	yī tóu N	"one (classifier) N" (used with things with heads, such as cattle)

A. There is overlap between the semantic properties that Navajo and Chinese grammaticalize. But now consider how English speakers would refer to certain objects in noun phrase constructions. Fill in an appropriate noun in the following English noun phrases:

1. five _sticks_ of chewing gum (note awkwardness of *five chewing gums*)

2. five _sticks_ of dynamite (note awkwardness of *five dynamites*)

3. five _pieces_ of coal (note awkwardness of *five coals*)

4. five _sheets_ of paper (note awkwardness of *five papers*)

5. five _head_ of cattle (note awkwardness of *five cattles*)

6. five _sticks_ of wood (note awkwardness of *five woods*)

B. Supply two more examples of the type of English noun phrase given in question A.

1. _____

2. _____

C. What Navajo verb root would you use when you handle

1. one piece of uncooked spaghetti _____

2. one piece of cooked spaghetti _____

3. a pot of cooked spaghetti _____

4. a handful of cooked spaghetti _____

D. Compare and contrast Chinese, Navajo, and English with respect to the importance that the physical shape of objects plays in constructing expressions in each language.

6 Language Variation

6.1 Abbreviated Questions

As in "tag-controlled deletion," an auxiliary verb (*do* in this case) can delete in yes/no questions. Study the sentences below and answer the questions that follow.

1a. Do you want some coffee?
 b. You want some coffee?

2a. Does she like the new dress?
 b. She like the new dress?

Questions

A. There is evidence that sentences 1b and 2b are "missing" the auxiliary verb *do*.

 3a.   You not want some coffee?
  b. *You not want some coffee.

 4a.   She not like the new dress?
  b. *She not like the new dress.

The occurrence of *not* is fine in the abbreviated yes/no questions (3a and 4a), whereas it is not in the declarative sentences (3b and 4b). Why is this so, and how does this provide evidence for the underlying occurrence of *do*? (Hint: Review *Linguistics*, pp. 145–150.)

B. The data in 5 and 6 provide further evidence for the presence of *do*.

5a. He want to leave?
 b. *He want to leave.
 c. He wants to leave.
 d. He does want to leave.
 e. Does he want to leave?

6a. Mary enjoy ice-skating?
 b. *Mary enjoy ice-skating.
 c. Mary enjoys ice-skating.
 d. Mary does enjoy ice-skating.
 e. Does Mary enjoy ice-skating?

The form of the verbs *want* and *enjoy* varies between *want/enjoy* and *wants/enjoys*. Discuss how this variation provides evidence for the "presence" of *do* in 5a and 6a. Cite the data from 5 and 6 in your discussion.

6.2 Pronouns: English

Questions

Answer the questions associated with each of the sentences below.

A. 1. Circle the pronoun you would prefer to use in each of the following sentences:

    a. Each senior believes that *they themselves/he himself/she herself* will graduate.

    b. One of the students will surely be on time, won't *they/she/he*?

    c. Each professor prepares *their own/his own/her own* syllabus.

  2. Consider sentences a–c again. Can you imagine situations where using the other pronoun(s) would be more appropriate? Describe them.

B. 1. Complete the sentences below by providing an appropriate tag.

    a. Everyone likes me, _____?

    b. Either John or Jane will go, _____?

    c. A pair of shoes is sitting there, _____?

    d. Everyone likes herself, _____?

2. Were any of your choices problematic? If so, which one(s) and why?

6.3 British English

The following passage contains many words and phrases characteristic of the British English spoken in London. As you read it, try to identify these words and phrases and their meaning in American English; then turn to the question that follows.

Nigel, wearing a smart lounge suit and carrying the inevitable waterproof, descended from the lift of his London flat and posted a letter in the pillarbox. Feeling hungry, Nigel turned into his favourite pub for a pint and some lunch. Bubble and squeak and bangers and mash did not appeal to him today. Instead, he chose plaice with potato. When he ordered, he learned that he had three choices of potato: chips, crisps, and jacket potato. He ordered the jacket potato with a side of courgettes and a slice of wholemeal bread.

After finishing lunch, Nigel walked onto the pavement and stopped to tighten his shoelaces. As he was passing a draper's shop, he suddenly remembered he needed something from a chemist. After having his order filled, he entered a call box, with the intention of calling his friend Llewellyn, since he had forgotten to call before he left his flat. He soon learned that the line was engaged, so he decided that if he was ever to catch Llewellyn up, he should have to take the Tube to Llewellyn's flat. Matters were not so simple since the IRA had phoned in bomb threats so the Tube was running late. The crowds around the buskers in the Tube did not help either.

On top of the Tube problem, it was a bank holiday. The shop assistants were walking with their boyfriends, and many of them were on their way to the cinemas. Matters were rather chaotic on the streets. Animal rights protesters were marching, and one had inadvertently stepped in front of a coach. He was taken to hospital in a critical condition.

Finally Nigel arrived at the flat of his friend Llewellyn. Because the day was bright, they decided to take a trip by train to Brighton and so booked a return. Since the trip was short, they only took monkeynuts and drinks. They read on the way, and a *Times* headline read, "England have won the soccer tournament." Also in the *Times* there was a report on Estuary English, a dialect which was having a major impact on London English. The two friends enjoyed the day and were glad to be out of the bustling city. (Revised from Blancké/Abraham 1935/1953, 49–50)

Question

Translate as much of the passage as you can into American English. Try to guess the meaning of each word that you do not know.

7 Language Change

7.1 Indo-European to English 1

By comparing historically related words in languages belonging to the Indo-European family, historians of language have reconstructed the Indo-European roots from which the daughter language words descended. Consider the following list of reconstructed Indo-European roots, along with their meanings, and answer questions A and B. (Note: In the context of historical linguistics, * denotes a reconstructed form, not an ungrammatical form.)

Indo-European root	English translation
1. *rendh-	"to tear up"
2. *rebh-	"to cover up"
3. *reug-	"to vomit; smoke, cloud"
4. *sab-	"juice"
5. *smer-	"grease, fat"
6. *webh-	"weave"
7. *ghrem-	"angry"
8. *dhelbh-	"to dig, excavate"
9. *del-	"to split, carve, cut"
10. *gleubh-	"to cut"
11. *kwed-	"to sharpen"
12. *kadh-	"to shelter, cover"

Questions

A. Associate the Indo-European words 1–12 with the historically related English words given on the next page. Assume that Grimm's Law (see appendix 6 and *Linguistics*, pp. 307–309) has applied in each appropriate case. The changes undergone by the vowels are much more complicated than the regular changes undergone by the consonants. Do not try to find a rule that expresses the changes undergone by the vowels. Simply try different vowels in the root until one fits. The regularity in the changes of the consonants and the similarity in the meanings provide enough information to determine uniquely which Indo-European root is the ancestor of the corresponding English word. Look at question B for additional help.

Indo-European root	English word
1. _____	hood
2. _____	sap
3. _____	rib
4. _____	whet
5. _____	grim
6. _____	reek
7. _____	delve
8. _____	cleave
9. _____	till
10. _____	rind
11. _____	web
12. _____	smear

B. Discuss informally how the meaning of each Indo-European root has changed to the meaning of its corresponding English word. Note that the Indo-European root is often given as a verb and the English word is a noun. Just work this meaning change into your answer. Example: The Indo-European root *kadh- "to cover, conceal" has become the English word *hood*. By Grimm's Law the *k* has become an *h* and the *dh* has become a *d*. The vowel *a* shows up as an *oo* /ʊ/. A *hood* is something that covers (and as a result partially conceals) the head and upper body. The *hood* of a car covers the engine. Thus, English *hood* preserves at least part of the meaning of its Indo-European ancestor *kadh-.

   1. *rendh-

   2. *rebh-

3. *reug-

4. *sab-

5. *smer-

6. *webh-

7. *ghrem-

8. *dhelbh-

9. *del-

10. *gleubh-

11. *kwed-

7.2 Indo-European to English 2

Below is a list of reconstructed Indo-European roots. Each root is paired with a Latin or Greek word that is descended from it. English translations of the Latin and Greek words are also given. Study the roots and their classical language cognates, and answer the question below. (Note: In the context of historical linguistics, * denotes a reconstructed form, not an ungrammatical form.)

Indo-European root	Classical language cognate
1. *gembh-	Greek: gomphos "tooth, peg, bolt"
2. *bhreu-	Latin: fervere "to be boiling or fermenting"
3. *kerp-(os-t)-	Greek: karpos "fruit"
4. *medh-(u)-	Greek: methu "wine"
5. *nog-(w)-	Latin: nudus "nude"
6. *pleu-	Latin: pluere "to rain"
7. *ruk-	Latin: ruga "wrinkle"
8. *spre(n)g-	Latin: spargere "to strew, scatter"
9. *spyeu-	Latin: spuere "to spit"
10. *steip-	Latin: stipare "to pack"

Question

Using the Latin and Greek words and their English glosses as hints, determine the Modern English cognates of the Indo-European roots 1–10. Apply Grimm's Law to the Indo-European roots to derive the corresponding Modern English consonants. (Note: Indo-European */p/, */t/, */k/ do not undergo Grimm's Law (i.e., they do not become /f/, /θ/, and /x/ (/h/), respectively) when they follow the consonant /s/.) The vowel correspondences between Indo-European and English are not so simple. Here you must use your imagination. Try different vowels, saying the word aloud, until you find a plausible English word that is related in *meaning* to the corresponding Latin or Greek word. Modern English spelling often reflects Old English pronunciation. This is an important clue you can use.

Indo-European root   English cognate

1. *gembh-   _____

2. *bhreu-   _____

3. *kerp-(os-t)- _____

4. *medh-(u)-   _____

5. *nog-(w)-   _____

6. *pleu-   _____

7. *ruk-   _____

8. *spre(n)g-   _____

9. *spyeu-   _____

10. *steip-   _____

8 Pragmatics

8.1 Identifying the Message

Look through cartoons A–J and answer the questions that follow.

A.

B.

C.

D.

E.

F.

G.

H.

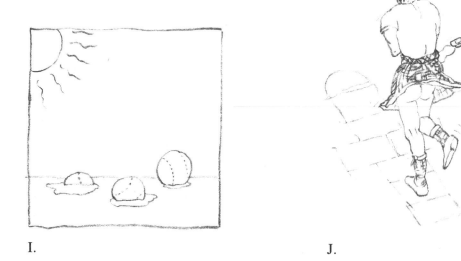

I.

J.

Questions

A. Match each caption with the most appropriate picture. In some cases the caption needs to be modified somewhat to make it appropriate (often this will involve recognizing ambiguities and/or homophony).

Captions	Cartoon
1. pitcher of beer	_____
2. butterballs	_____
3. royal pain	_____
4. hopscotch	_____
5. bird dog	_____
6. catfish	_____
7. fly-by-night	_____
8. a tale of two cities	_____
9. rugby	_____
10. Popeye	_____

B. Discuss possible problems each expression in question A poses for the Message Model of linguistic communication. (See appendix 7 and chapter 9 of *Linguistics* for discussion of the Message Model.)

1.

2.

3.

4.

5.

6.

7.

8.

9.

10.

8.2 Communication Breakdown

Study the cartoon and answer questions A–C.

Questions

A. In *Linguistics*, pp. 354–359, the strategies for literal and direct communication are outlined. At what stage has communication broken down?

B. Given the context of utterance, is it likely that communication would indeed break down? Why or why not?

C. If you argued in question B that it is unlikely that communication would have broken down, then discuss the following question: Does the Message Model have any way of capturing the unlikelihood of communication breaking down in this kind of case? Why or why not? (Review *Linguistics*, pp. 346–351.)

8.3 Literal/Nonliteral Use

Question

A speaker could utter each of the following sentences with the intention of communicating either literally or nonliterally. For at least five of them, state at least two meanings (at least one of which should be literal and at least one of which should be nonliteral) that a speaker could have in mind in using the sentence.

For example: *They are on the way out.* (1) *They* refers to some people who are leaving the room. (2) *They* refers to some shoes that were fashionable last fall but are going out of style.

1. He is on the edge.
2. We're in the same boat.
3. I have my hands full.
4. He didn't get to first base.
5. She broke his heart.
6. That will keep them on their toes.
7. She's losing her grip.
8. He flew off the handle.
9. She blew off steam.
10. Barbara got under her skin.
11. Sue is tied up.
12. He refused to lay his cards on the table.
13. She bit Mary's head off.
14. She gives it to him straight.
15. They beat their brains out.
16. That rings a bell.
17. I got the picture.
18. He'll change his tune.
19. That is right up my alley.
20. He is on the ball.
21. She is standing on her own two feet.
22. He always takes it with a grain of salt.
23. My father is a wet blanket.
24. He will sink or swim.
25. You took the words right out of my mouth.
26. That movie was a real turkey!

1. a.

   b.

2. a.

   b.

3. a.

   b.

4. a.

   b.

5. a.

   b.

228

8.4 Indirectness

Indirectness in communication involves performing one linguistic act by means of performing another linguistic act. For example, one can perform the act of "ordering" by way of "stating." In answering the questions below, you will be exploring this and other indirect linguistic acts. (See *Linguistics*, pp. 363–367.)

Questions

A. Examine sentences 1–5 and discuss in each case how the speaker could be using the sentence indirectly.

For example: *The bill comes to $10.29.* This sentence is in the declarative mood. (Concerning moods, see appendix 8.) Either it is true that the bill comes to $10.29, or it is false. But one can imagine a situation where someone uttering this sentence (a waiter) could be taken as *requesting* someone else (a customer) to pay the sum of $10.29. That is, it is appropriate on hearing this sentence for the hearer not just to take note of the amount of the bill, but to do something (pay the bill). This is therefore an instance of indirection: performing one act (requesting) by way of another act (stating).

1. I'm hungry.

2. The children are asleep.

3. Are you done yet?

4. What time is it?

5. Is that the radio again?

B. Indirectness can also involve "questioning" by way of "ordering." That is, the sentence is in the imperative mood, but the speaker is also asking for information and is not merely ordering. List some examples of this kind of indirectness.

C. A third form of indirectness involves "stating" by way of "commanding." That is, the sentence is in the imperative mood, but the speaker is also making a statement. List some examples of this kind of indirectness.

8.5 Tag Questions: English

As noted in *Linguistics*, pp. 147–150, 155, 272–275, tags can occur in positive or negative forms:

1a. Herman is wanting to leave, *is* he!
 b. Herman is wanting to leave, *isn't* he?

2a. You know you're smart, *do* you!
 b. You know you're smart, *don't* you?

3a. I owe you an apology, *do* I!
 b. I owe you an apology, *don't* I?

Questions

A. How do the positive and negative tags differ in their use? That is, when would you use the positive tag but not the negative tag, and vice versa?

B. Provide additional pairs of examples like the ones above in order to support your answer.

231

8.6 "Unclear Reference" of Pronouns: English

In this exercise you will be trying to figure out the nature of a particular problem: an example of what has been described in a college handbook on writing as "unclear reference" of a pronoun. The handbook characterizes the problem in grammatical terms (see question A). The data in questions B–D challenge this conclusion.

Questions

A. In *Writing: A College Handbook*, the authors offer examples of what they call "unclear reference." One example is as follows:

1. A recent editorial contained an attack on the medical profession. The writer accused them of charging excessively high fees.

The authors provide the following discussion:

Who is meant by the pronoun *them*? From the phrase *medical profession* you may guess that the writer is referring to doctors. But *profession* cannot be the antecedent of *them*, for *them* is plural and *profession* is singular. (Heffernan and Lincoln 1982, 309)

Now consider examples 2 and 3 and answer questions A-1 through A-5.

2. Yesterday, the President announced the decision to send aid to numerous countries in Central America. He went on to say that it was time to help our neighbors in this hemisphere.
3. Yesterday, the White House announced the decision to lift all sanctions. He went on to say that this gesture would set the tone for further negotiations.

1. Who is *he* in example 2?

2. Assume that the noun phrase "antecedent" for *he* is *the White House* in example 3. Who would you guess *he* is? (You may think of several possibilities.)

3. In order to answer question A-2, what kinds of issues must you consider?

4. Examples 2 and 3 are similar in that in each example both the noun phrase "antecedent" (*the President* and *the White House*, respectively) and the pronoun *he* are singular. How are these examples *dissimilar* with respect to determining the reference of *he*?

5. In example 3 *the White House* and the pronoun *he* are both singular, whereas the college handbook describes the problem of determining the reference of *them* in example 1 as a problem of number incompatibility (*profession* is singular, whereas *them* is plural; therefore, *profession* cannot be the "antecedent" for *them*). Is number compatibility between the noun phrase "antecedent" and the pronoun sufficient for determining the reference of the pronoun? Explain, using examples 1 and 3 to back up your arguments.

B. Now consider example 4 and answer questions B-1 through B-4.

4. The office threw a surprise birthday party for the boss. They even gave her a beautiful gift.

1. Who are *they* and how do you know?

2. Is the noun phrase "antecedent" of *they* singular or plural?

3. How does this bear on your discussion in question A-5?

4. Who is *her* being used to refer to? How do you know?

C. The authors of *Writing* suggest that because the pronoun *they* in example 1 is plural, it cannot have the singular *medical profession* as its antecedent, hence that the referent has essentially not been introduced and is therefore indeterminate. Although the reference of the pronoun in this example may indeed be "vague," we must ask whether this problem is to be properly characterized in grammatical terms. Sentence-*internally* we can see that the grammatical requirement of number "agreement" does play a role. Compare example 1 with examples 5 and 6.

5a. *The doctor pays themselves well.

  b. The doctor pays herself well.

6a. *The medical profession pays themselves well.

  b. The medical profession pays itself well.

1. Both examples 5a and 6a are ungrammatical. Identify the problem, keeping in mind examples 1–3.

2. Describe any differences you notice between examples 5a and 6a.

D. Now consider examples 7–9 and answer the questions that follow.

7. They entered the beauty salon and had their hair done.

8. They're flying south for the winter early this year.

9. They won't graduate in four years if they keep up like that.

1. None of the examples in 7–9 provides a noun phrase "antecedent" for the pronoun *they*. Can you guess what the reference of *they* might be in each case?

2. What kind of information did you rely on to make your guesses in question D-1?

3. Does the kind of information you used in question D-2 play a role in helping to identify the reference of the pronoun *they* in example 1? Discuss.

E. In your opinion, is there a problem with the reference of the pronoun *them* in example 1? If your answer is "yes," then discuss why number incompatibility between the noun phrase "antecedent" and the pronoun cannot be the explanation for the problem. If your answer is "no," then explain why the college handbook discussion is inappropriate for you.

8.7 Performative Verbs versus Perlocutionary Verbs

A *performative utterance* describes the act being performed. For example, in the sentence *I predict that it will rain* the performative verb *predict* names the act of predicting; given the right beliefs and intentions, the speaker could, in uttering this sentence, be making a prediction. A *perlocutionary utterance*, on the other hand, is intended to include an effect on the hearer. For example, in the sentence *She persuaded Mary that the argument was solid*, the perlocutionary verb *persuade* describes an act of causing someone to believe or do something (in this case, the act of causing Mary to believe that the argument was solid). In certain syntactic environments the presence of a perlocutionary verb yields an oddity. For example, it is odd to say *I (hereby) persuade you to leave*.

Examine sentences 1–10, and answer the questions that follow.

1. I (hereby) promise to be there.
2. I (hereby) suggest that you leave.
3. I (hereby) convince you that I am right.
4. I (hereby) warn you not to come any closer.
5. I (hereby) incite you to be angry.
6. I (hereby) forbid you to enter this room.
7. I (hereby) inspire you to write beautiful music.
8. I (hereby) amuse you with this story.
9. I (hereby) order you to be quiet.
10. I (hereby) provoke you to punch me.

Questions

A. Which underlined verbs in 1–10 are performative verbs? Give your reasons.

239

B. Which underlined verbs in 1–10 are perlocutionary verbs? Give your reasons.

C. *I hereby persuade you to leave* is odd. Why is this so? That is, try to *explain* the nature of the oddity.

8.8 Proverbs

Consider the following proverbs and answer questions A and B.

1. Each bird loves to hear himself sing.
2. Friendship is not to be bought at a fair.
3. Fruit ripens not well in the shade.
4. Full bellies make empty skulls.
5. Forbidden fruit is sweet.
6. Fools live poor to die rich.
7. Every tide hath its ebb.
8. Fame is a magnifying glass.
9. Every bird likes its own nest the best.
10. Every bird must hatch its own eggs.
11. What goes around comes around.
12. Can a mouse fall in love with a cat?

Questions

A. How would you paraphrase the intended message behind five of the above proverbs?

1.

2.

3.

4.

5.

B. What kinds of communicative uses of language do proverbs exemplify? In what sense, if any, are proverbs nonliteral? Defend your answer. Discuss at least five of the proverbs.

8.9 Pronoun/Antecedent Agreement: English

The following "agreement principle" can be found in *College Entrance Reviews in English Composition* (revised 1971). Study "Principle 9" and answer the questions that follow.

Principle 9. The number of a pronoun is determined by its antecedent. *Every, each, everyone, anybody, no one,* etc., are singular antecedents. In most instances, in order to avoid awkwardness, *he* or *his* is used to denote both masculine and feminine genders.

1. If *anybody* is looking for an exciting plot, let *him* (not *them*) read this book.
2. *Every one of them* spoke up for *his* own point of view.
3. *Every girl and every boy* in the class is making *his* oral report on the supplementary book today.

Questions

A. Under the view expressed in Principle 9 it is "incorrect" to write a sentence like example 4.

4. Every one of them spoke up for their own point of view.

Nonetheless, examples such as 4 are certainly common these days. Ask your peers whether examples 5 and 6 sound "okay" or not and record your results.

5. Anyone who thinks they can graduate in two years without working is either a genius or out of touch.
6. Somebody in the house left the lights on, didn't they?

B. If consultants say that examples 5 and 6 sound "okay," ask them whether they find any difference between examples 5–6 and examples 7–8 (e.g., differences in use, differences in what the speaker may have in mind, contextual appropriateness). Record your results.

7. Anyone who thinks he can graduate in two years without working is either a genius or out of touch.
8. Somebody in the house left the lights on, didn't he?

C. How does the following quotation from *The First Twelve Months of Life* (1985) bear on the use of *they/them* versus *he/him*? Why would the author include such a comment in the introduction of his book?

A word about gender. Writers on child care may some day succeed in introducing into the language a word that means both "he" and "she." Meantime we will use the convention of the masculine pronoun, but we assure you that unless we are talking about something where sex makes a difference, everything we say about "him" refers to your new daughter as well.

8.10 Major Moods 1: English

Different languages have different ways of signaling the major moods (declarative, interrogative, imperative). In this exercise and the three that follow, you will explore the syntactic, morphological, and phonological devices that languages use to mark these classes of speech acts. (For a discussion of major moods, see appendix 8.)

Each English sentence below is associated with one of the three major moods. Examine the data, and answer questions A–D.

1. Eat your spinach!
2. Tom left the room.
3. Did Tom leave the room?
4. Tom left the room?
5. Mary likes fish.
6. Mary likes fish?
7. Does Mary like fish?
8. Who likes fish?

9. What does Mary like?
10. Pass the salt!
11. John is turning down the radio.
12. John is turning down the radio?
13. Is John turning down the radio?
14. Turn down the radio!
15. Who turned the radio down?
16. What did you eat?

Questions

A. 1. Which sentences are in the interrogative mood? That is, which ones are associated with the answerhood condition? List them by number.

2. What is the nature of the grammatical form that signals the interrogative mood? (Noting the use of the question mark ("?") is not an acceptable answer.)

3. Do yes/no questions have anything in common syntactically with some *wh*-questions (questions formed with the words *who(m)*, *what*, etc.)? (Compare examples 3, 9, 13, and 16.)

B. 1. Which sentences are in the imperative mood? That is, which ones are associated with the compliance condition? List them by number.

2. What is the nature of the grammatical form that signals the imperative mood? (Noting the use of the exclamation mark ("!") is not an acceptable answer.)

C. 1. Which sentences are in the declarative mood? That is, which sentences are associated with a truth condition? List them by number.

2. What is the nature of the grammatical form that signals the declarative mood? (Noting the use of the period (".") is not an acceptable answer.)

D. What kinds of grammatical devices does English use to signal mood? That is, what syntactic, morphological, and phonological properties of a sentence function to signal mood?

8.11 Major Moods 2: Finnish

The following declarative, interrogative, and imperative sentences are from Finnish, a European language that is not a member of the Indo-European language family. Consider the Finnish sentences and their English translations, and answer questions A–D.

Finnish words exhibit vowel harmony. Thus, the vowels in suffixes vary, depending on the quality of the vowels of the words to which they are attached. In this exercise certain suffixes will therefore appear in two different forms, but they are to be considered as two different versions of the same morpheme. The vowel *ä* is a low front unrounded vowel; the vowel *ö* is a mid front rounded vowel; and the vowel *y* is a high front rounded vowel. A sequence of two identical vowels represents a long vowel of the same quality. (Hint: One way of marking the third person singular subject in Finnish is by lengthening the final vowel of the verb.)

The words in parentheses are optional.

Finnish sentence	English gloss
1. He juovat maitoa hitaasti.	"They are drinking milk slowly."
2. Haluanko (minä) teetä?	"Do I want tea?"
3. Rouva Joki pitää kahvista.	"Mrs. Joki likes coffee."
4. Syö kalaa!	"Eat fish!" (familiar sg.)
5. Juovatko he olutta?	"Are they drinking beer?"
6. (Minä) tarvitsen kupit tänä iltana.	"I need the cups tonight."
7. Juovatko he maitoa hitaasti?	"Are they drinking milk slowly?"
8. Hän haluaa kahvia.	"He/She wants coffee."
9. (Minä) haluan mehua.	"I want (some) juice."
10. (Sinä) juot maitoa tänä iltana.	"You are drinking milk this evening."
11. Pitääkö Rouva Joki kahvista?	"Does Mrs. Joki like coffee?"
12. Haluaako hän kahvia?	"Does he/she want coffee?"
13. Juokaa teetä!	"Drink tea!" (formal sg. or familiar pl.)
14. Tarvitsenko (minä) kupit tänä iltana?	"Do I need cups tonight?"
15. Syökää kalaa!	"Eat fish!" (formal sg. or familiar pl.)
16. Juoko hän nyt olutta?	"Is he/she drinking beer now?"
17. Juo olutta!	"Drink (some) beer!" (familiar sg.)
18. (Minä) haluan teetä.	"I want (some) tea."
19. Hän juo nyt olutta.	"He/She is drinking beer now."
20. Juotko (sinä) maitoa tänä iltana?	"Are you drinking milk tonight?"
21. Haluanko (minä) mehua?	"Do I want (some) juice?"

22. Juo teetä!	"Drink tea!" (familiar sg.)
23. Mikä tämä on?	"What is this?"
24. Tämä on kirja.	"This is a book."
25. Missä kirja on?	"Where is the book?"
26. Missä kahvi on?	"Where is the coffee?"
27. Kuka Tuomari Brown on?	"Who is Judge Brown?"
28. Hän on amerikkalainen diplomaattii.	"He is an American diplomat."
29. Kuka tarvitsee kupit tänä iltana?	"Who needs the cups this evening?"
30. Mitä (partitive case) Tuomari Brown syöö?	"What does Judge Brown eat?"
31. Kenet (objective case) (sinä) tarvitset tänä iltana?	"Who(m) do you need tonight?"

Questions

A. How is person marked in Finnish? That is, by what means are first person (*I*), second person (*you*), and so forth, marked?

B. Compare and contrast the formation of Finnish yes/no questions with the formation of English yes/no questions. Finnish yes/no questions have the same intonation patterns as Finnish declarative sentences. Both have a slight fall in intonation at the end of the sentence.

C. Compare and contrast the formation of Finnish questions that use interrogative pronouns (i.e., pronouns such as *who(m)* and *what*) with the formation of corresponding English questions. Finnish questions with interrogative pronouns have the same intonation patterns as declarative sentences.

D. Compare and contrast the formation of Finnish imperative sentences with that of English imperative sentences.

8.12 Major Moods 3: Copala Trique

Below are sentences illustrating the declarative, interrogative, and imperative moods in Copala Trique, an Otomanguean language spoken in Mexico. Analyze the sentences, and answer questions A–D.

Copala Trique has five phonemic tones, indicated by the numerals 1–5. Vowels marked with 1 (e.g., a^1) are uttered with lowest pitch; those marked with 5 are uttered with highest pitch. Sequences of numbers represent tone contours on individual vowels. For example, a 13 sequence is a tone contour that rises in pitch.

The phonetic symbols used in this exercise are given in the chart in appendix 3. The only symbol that does not appear in the chart is !. This symbol represents a feature of articulation, the details of which are too complicated to discuss here (but see Rensch 1978). Familiarity with the phonetic properties of these symbols is not necessary for analyzing the sentences and answering the questions.

	Copala Trique sentence	English gloss
1.	Ki²ya¹³h či³ we³² a³².	"The man will build a house."
2.	Turu²no⁴! či³ we³² a³².	"The man will paint a house."
3.	Turu²no⁴! ša³na¹! we³² a³².	"The woman will paint a house."
4.	Turu²no⁴! ša³na¹! me³sa⁴! a³².	"The woman will paint a table."
5.	Ki²ya¹³h ša³na¹! me³sa⁴! a³².	"The woman will make a table."
6.	Ki²ya¹³h či³ we³² adõh².	"The man will surely build a house."
7.	Ki²ya¹³h ša³na¹! me³sa⁴! na⁴².	"Will the woman make a table?"
8.	Turu²no⁴! či³ me³sa⁴! na⁴².	"Will the man paint a table?"
9.	Ki²ya¹³h ša³na¹! we³² ža²².	"The woman will build a house, won't she?"
10.	Ki²ya¹³h zo³h we³² a³².	"You all will build a house."
11.	Ki²ya¹³h zo³h we³² a⁴.	"Build a house (you all)!"
12.	Turu²no⁴! zo³h me³sa⁴! a⁴.	"Paint a table (you all)!"
13.	Me³! zi⁵ turu²no⁴! we³² ga².	"Who will paint a house?"
14.	Me³! zi⁵ ki²ya¹³h me³sa⁴! ga².	"Who will make a table?"
15.	Me³! ze³²! ki²ya¹³h či³ ga².	"What will the man make?"
16.	Me³! ze³²! turu²no⁴! ša³na¹! ga².	"What will the woman paint?"
17.	Ka²ã³²h šni³ šumã³² a³².	"The boy went to town."
18.	Ka²ã³²h šni³ šumã³² na⁴².	"Did the boy go to town?"
19.	Ka²ã³²h či³ šumã³² a³².	"The man went to town."
20.	Ka²ã³²h či³ šumã³² na⁴².	"Did the man go to town?"
21.	Ka²ã³²h zo¹² šumã³² a⁴.	"Go to town!" (sg.)
22.	Kanã²h zo¹² a⁴.	"Weave!" (sg.)

23. Kunã²h zo¹ʔ a⁴.   "Run away!" (sg.)
24. Keneʔe³! ša³na¹! (mã³!) šni³ a³².   "The woman saw the boy."
25. Keneʔe³! šni³ (mã³!) ša³na¹! a³².   "The boy saw the woman."
26. Me³! zi⁵ keneʔe³! šni³ ga².   "Who(m) did the boy see?"
27. Me³! zi⁵ keneʔe³! mã³! šni³ ga².   "Who saw the boy?"
28. Me³! zi⁵ kaʔã³²h šumã³ʔ ga².   "Who went to town?"
29. Me³! zi⁵ ča⁴! ru³ci¹ʔ ga².   "Who ate the guava?"
30. Me³! ze³²! keneʔe³! či³ ga².   "What did the man see?"
31. Me³! ze³²! ča⁴! ša³na¹! ga².   "What did the woman eat?"

Questions

A. How are Copala Trique yes/no questions formed?

B. How are Copala Trique questions with interrogative words (in English *who*, *what*, etc., which are called *wh-words*) formed? Compare and contrast the formation of Copala Trique interrogative word questions with the formation of English interrogative word questions.

C. How are Copala Trique imperative sentences formed?

D. Discuss the role of word order in Copala Trique. In particular, discuss the absence versus presence of the word $m\tilde{a}^3!$ in sentences 26 and 27, respectively.

8.13 Major Moods 4: Mandarin Chinese

The following sentences illustrate the form that the major moods take in Mandarin Chinese. Analyze the sentences, and answer questions A–D.

Chinese is a tone language; that is, each word is uttered at a characteristic pitch level or with a characteristic pitch change. The tones are indicated with diacritic marks over the vowels. The diacritic ‾ over a vowel indicates a high tone; the diacritic ′ indicates a rising tone; the diacritic ˘ indicates a falling-rising tone; the diacritic ` indicates a falling tone.

Mandarin Chinese sentence	English gloss
1. Tā shì jiàoyuán.	"He is a teacher."
2. (Nǐ) mǎi shū!	"Buy the books!"
3. Nǐ yào shén-mo?	"What do you want?"
4. Tā bù dào Měi-guo lái.	"He is not coming to America."
5. Wáng-Xiānsheng lái ma?	"Is Mr. Wang coming?"
6. Wáng-Xiānsheng lái.	"Mr. Wang is coming."
7. Nǐ yǒu shū ma?	"Do you have any books?"
8. Sheí mài bǐ?	"Who sells pens?"
9. Wǒ yǒu shū.	"I have books."
10. (Nǐ) kàn tā-men!	"Look at them!"
11. Zhè shì shén-mo?	"What is this?"
12. Wǒ-men shuō Zhōng-guo-huà.	"We speak Chinese."
13. Tā-men shuō bù shuō Zhōng-guo-huà?	"Do they speak Chinese?"
14. (Nǐ) shuō Zhōng-guo-huà!	"Speak Chinese!"
15. Nǐ-men mài bù mài bǐ?	"Do you (pl.) sell pens?"
16. Tā-men mài bǐ ma?	"Do they sell pens?"
17. Zhè shì shū.	"This is a book."
18. (Nǐ) lái!	"Come!"
19. Wǒ yào mǎi shū.	"I want to buy books."
20. Nǐ kàn wǒ ma?	"Are you looking at me?"
21. Tā-men bù wèn wǒ-men.	"They didn't ask us."
22. Nǐ-men kàn sheí?	"Who(m) did you (pl.) look at?"
23. Nǐ shì bù shì jiàoyuán?	"Are you a teacher?"
24. Tā-men bù kàn wǒ-men.	"They are not looking at us."
25. Wǒ bù kàn nǐ-men.	"I am not looking at you."

Questions

A. 1. Which sentences are in the interrogative mood? That is, which ones are associated with the answerhood condition? List them by number.

   2. Describe two ways in which yes/no questions can be formed in Chinese.

   3. How are *wh*-questions formed in Chinese? (In English, *wh*-questions are those formed with interrogative pronouns such as *who(m)*, *what*, and so forth.)

B. 1. Which sentences are in the imperative mood? That is, which ones are associated with the compliance condition? List them by number.

   2. What is the nature of the grammatical form that signals the imperative mood in Chinese?

C. Which sentences are in the declarative mood? That is, which ones are associated with a truth condition? List them by number.

D. Does word order appear to be important in Chinese? Be specific.

8.14 Pragmatics: Navajo

Some of the following Navajo sentences are acceptable; others (marked with #) are judged by native speakers to be pragmatically unacceptable. In list I both sentences in each pair are acceptable; in lists II and III one sentence in each pair is acceptable and the other is pragmatically odd. Study the sentence pairs in the three lists, and answer the question at the end of the exercise.

There are two differences between the sentences in each pair: a word order change between the first two words (nouns) and a morphological change in the last word (the verb). When the verb begins with *y-* (more precisely, *yi-*), the first noun is the subject. When the verb begins with *bi-*, the second noun is the subject. The pairs of Navajo sentences have been translated into active and passive forms in English, although the sentences translated as English passives are not really passive sentences in Navajo. However, understanding the exact nature of this structural type in Navajo is not important for completing the exercise.

Not all transitive sentences in Navajo have acceptable pairs with the prefixes *yi-* and *bi-*. In list II the *bi-* form yields a pragmatic oddity; in list III the *yi-* form is pragmatically unacceptable.

We have not provided interlinear glosses in lists II and III, since you will know enough about Navajo syntax from studying list I to figure out the meaning of the Navajo words from the English translations.

List I

	Navajo sentence	English gloss
1a.	Łį́į' dzaanééz yiztał. horse mule kicked	"The horse kicked the mule."
b.	Dzaanééz łį́į' biztał.	"The mule was kicked by the horse."
2a.	Tł'ízí dibé yizgoh. goat sheep butted	"The goat butted the sheep."
b.	Dibé tł'ízí bizgoh.	"The sheep was butted by the goat."
3a.	Ashkii at'ééd yizts'ǫs. boy girl kissed	"The boy kissed the girl."
b.	At'ééd ashkii bizts'ǫs.	"The girl was kissed by the boy."
4a.	Łééchąą'í másí yishxash. dog cat bit	"The dog bit the cat."
b.	Másí łééchąą'í bishxash.	"The cat was bitten by the dog."

5a. Hastiin asdzání yiyiiłts'ą́.
man woman saw
"The man saw the woman."

b. Asdzání hastiin biiłts'ą́.
"The woman was seen by the man."

6a. Hastiin ashkii yizloh.
man boy roped
"The man roped the boy."

b. Ashkii hastiin bizloh.
"The boy was roped by the man."

7a. Ma'ii dibé yiyiisxį́.
coyote sheep killed
"The coyote killed the sheep."

b. Dibé ma'ii biisxį́.
"The sheep was killed by the coyote."

8a. Mósí łééchąą'í yizghas.
cat dog scratched
"The cat scratched the dog."

b. Łééchąą'í mósí bizghas.
"The dog was scratched by the cat."

List II

9a. Łį́į́' tsé yiztał.
"The horse kicked the rock."
b. #Tsé łį́į́' biztał.
"The rock was kicked by the horse."

10a. Mósí abe' yiłch'al.
"The cat is lapping the milk."
b. #Abe' mósí biłch'al.
"The milk is being lapped by the cat."

11a. Łééchąą'í łeets'aa' yiłnaad.
"The dog licks the dish."
b. #Łeets'aa' łééchąą'í biłnaad.
"The dish is licked by the dog."

12a. Mósí naaltsoos yizghas.
"The cat scratches the paper."
b. #Naaltsoos mósí bizghas.
"The paper is scratched by the cat."

13a. Dibé tł'oh yiłchozh.
"The sheep eats the grass."
b. #Tł'oh dibé biłchozh.
"The grass is eaten by the sheep."

14a. Ashkii naaltsoos yizhjih.
"The boy grabbed the book."
b. #Naaltsoos ashkii bizhjih.
"The book was grabbed by the boy."

15a. Ashkii tsé'édó'ii yik'idiiltáál.
"The boy stepped on the fly."
b. #Tsé'édó'ii ashkii bik'idiiltáál.
"The fly was stepped on by the boy."

16a. Ashkii bįįh yiskah.
"The boy shot the deer."
b. #Bįįh ashkii biskah.
"The deer was shot by the boy."

17a. At'ééd dibé yizloh.
"The girl roped the sheep."
b. #Dibé at'ééd bizloh.
"The sheep was roped by the girl."

18a. Ashkii gah yisił.
"The boy caught the rabbit."
b. #Gah ashkii bisił.
"The rabbit was caught by the boy."

List III

19a. #Tsah asdzání yaa'íijil.
"The needle stuck the woman."
b. Asdzání tsah baa'íijil.
"The woman was stuck by the needle."

20a. #Béésh ashkii yizhgish.
"The knife cut the boy."
b. Ashkii béésh bizhgish.
"The boy was cut by the knife."

21a. #Wóláchíí' hastiin yishish.
"The red ant stung the man."
b. Hastiin wóláchíí' bishish.
"The man was stung by the red ant."

260

22a. #Ts'í'ii łį́į' yiyííts'ǫ́ǫz.   "The mosquito sucked on the horse."
 b.   Łį́į' ts'í'ii bííts'ǫ́ǫz.   "The horse was sucked on by the
                 mosquito."

Question

Using the sentences in lists I, II, and III, determine the principle(s) that explain why some of the sentences are unacceptable to Navajo speakers. Be sure to consider the referents of the NPs with respect to the grammatical relations they hold.

9 Psychology of Language

9.1 Speech Errors

The phrases and sentences 1–12 illustrate various types of speech errors. Read them, and answer the question that follows. (Some of the examples are taken from Fromkin 1973, Foss and Hakes 1978, and Garrett 1975.)

1. when the bare gets all ground   (as in autumn)
2. Stocks stay up.   (refers to an article of clothing)
3. Seymour sliced the knife with a salami.
4. The early worm gets the bird.
5. Fire fighters are helping to put out blazers.
6. mushmallows   (hint: a fungus and a confection)
7. taddle tennis
8. budbegs
9. foon speeding
10. Make it so the apple has less trees.
11. bridge of the neck
12. The legislature is in its final week of law-breaking.

Question

Discuss the nature of each speech error. Point out whether the error involves phonology, morphology, syntax, or a combination of any of these. That is, what type of unit is involved? What expression was intended in each case?

1. a. Type of error:

   b. Linguistic unit involved:

   c. Intended expression:

2. a.

   b.

   c.

3. a.

   b.

   c.

4. a.

   b.

   c.

5. a.

   b.

   c.

6. a.

   b.

   c.

7. a.

   b.

   c.

8. a.

   b.

   c.

9. a.

   b.

   c.

10. a.

    b.

    c.

11. a.

    b.

    c.

12. a.

    b.

    c.

Appendixes

1 How to State Phonological Rules

Several exercises in this workbook require an informal statement of some phonological rule(s). These rules express regularities in the patterning of the sounds in the language in question. In this appendix we will demonstrate how to state such rules, using examples from English.

Consider the following regularity in the pronunciation of vowels in American English: vowels are longer when they appear before voiced consonants than when they appear before voiceless ones. To perceive this difference, utter the words *bit* and *bid* a few times. Notice how much longer the vowel lasts in *bid* than it does in *bit*. The conditioning factor for the lengthening of the vowel in this case is the voiced sound *d* that follows it. A similar length difference appears in the words *tap* and *tab*. Even the already long or tense vowels in pairs such as *beat* and *bead* show a relative length difference.

This lengthening rule of American English vowels is thus a condition on pronunciation that every native speaker has learned. The regularity describing vowel length can be expressed in statement 1.

1. A vowel is lengthened before a voiced consonant.

This statement can also be expressed in the following more concise notation:

2. [vowel] → [lengthened] / ____ [voiced consonants]

And this statement in turn is an instance of a more abstract rule pattern:

3. A → B / C ____ D

Rule pattern 3 can be read as follows: "A is realized as B when it appears in an environment where it is immediately preceded by C (i.e., A is to the right of C) and immediately followed by D (i.e., A is to the left of D)."

In other words:

→   is to be read "is realized as" or "becomes."
/   is to be read "in the environment of."
____   (called the *focus bar*) specifies the relative position of the segment subject to the rule, in this case A, to the segments conditioning the rule, in this case C and D.

The pattern given in rule schema 3 is characteristic of most of the phonological regularities found in this workbook and is typical of the pattern of phonological rules found in the world's languages.

In the case of the American English vowel-lengthening rule, A is any vowel, B is the specification "lengthening," C is lacking, and D is a voiced consonant. This is the form given as rule statement 2.

An example of a phonological rule in which both C and D must be present is the Flap Rule (see *Linguistics*, p. 84), which specifies that a flap, [D], replaces a [t] when it occurs between vowels and when the first vowel is stressed:

4. [t] → [D] / [V́] ____ [V]

This rule is characteristic of modern American English. It accounts for the pronunciation of *pitted* [pʰɪDɨd] and *hottest* [hɔDəst]. It is, then, an example of rule template 3 in which A is *t*, B is the flapped *D*, C is a stressed vowel, and D is another vowel.

There are also rules in which part C of the conditioning environment is present and part D is absent. An example is the Plural Rule of English (see *Linguistics*, pp. 78–82).

2 The Role of Distinctive Features in Phonological Rules

For the most part, phonological rules can be expressed with a formula of the form A → B / C ____ D, where the alphabetic symbols represent one or more phonemes (see appendix 1). However, since the smallest isolatable units of a language's sound system are not phonemes (or their allophones), but the distinctive features that compose the phonemes, phonological rules are better stated in terms of these distinctive features.

To begin to see why this is so, let us return to the Vowel-Lengthening Rule of English discussed in appendix 1:

1. English Vowel-Lengthening Rule
   [vowel] → [lengthened] / ____ [voiced consonants]

The form of rule 1 already anticipates the point that such rules are best expressed in terms of the distinctive features that make up the phonemes that participate in the phonological regularities of a language. Contrast rule 1 with the same rule expressed in terms of phonemes:

$$
2.\
\begin{bmatrix}
\text{I} \\ \varepsilon \\ \text{æ} \\ \Lambda \\ \text{ɑ} \\ \text{ɔ} \\ \text{U} \\ \text{iy} \\ \text{ey} \\ \text{ay} \\ \text{uw} \\ \text{ow} \\ \text{aw} \\ \text{oy}
\end{bmatrix}
\rightarrow
\begin{bmatrix}
\text{I:} \\ \varepsilon\text{:} \\ \text{æ:} \\ \Lambda\text{:} \\ \text{ɑ:} \\ \text{ɔ:} \\ \text{U:} \\ \text{i:y} \\ \text{e:y} \\ \text{a:y} \\ \text{u:w} \\ \text{o:w} \\ \text{a:w} \\ \text{o:y}
\end{bmatrix}
/\ \underline{\quad}\
\begin{bmatrix}
\text{b} \\ \text{d} \\ \text{g} \\ \text{m} \\ \text{n} \\ \text{ŋ} \\ \text{v} \\ \text{ð} \\ \text{z} \\ \text{ž} \\ \text{ǰ} \\ \text{r} \\ \text{l}
\end{bmatrix}
$$

Although rules 1 and 2 account for the same data, rule 1 expresses the generalization that explains *why* the phonemes that are listed in rule 2 pattern together. For example, as far as the list of phonemes in rule 2 is concerned, we could replace *z* with *s* on the right (part D of the context), and rule 2 would be almost the same in form and complexity. Only rule 1 explains why *s* is excluded in part D of the rule, however: *s* is a voiceless consonant, and all of the other consonants in the right-hand list in rule 2 are voiced. Rule 1 *rules out* the presence of *s* in the list of conditioning phonemes—exactly the right result.

In addition, the formulation of rule 1 makes unnecessary the large number of individual statements that would be required if we were forced (for some reason) to make all of the allophonic statements for each phoneme individually. Clearly, we would not want to have a rule stating that the phoneme /ɪ/ has a variant [ɪ:] before *d*, *n*, *z*, and so forth. It is not the case that each phoneme of a language must have its own individual sets of rules that determine its allophones; rather, rules that specify allophonic detail are general and may be applicable to several phonemes.

As it is now stated, rule 1 is not precisely in the form in which phonological rules must be written. Two changes are needed: first, the specifications + (plus) and − (minus) must be added to the features; and second, a more precise and empirically justified set of distinctive features must be employed. For justification of the intrinsic content of a more appropriate set of distinctive features, see *Linguistics*, pp. 100–108.

We have already tacitly assumed that the features that make up phonemes are binary. That is, each one can have two values: + and −. For example, the feature of voicing can appear either as voiced ([+voiced]) or as voiceless ([−voiced]). There are two reasons for claiming that distinctive features are binary. First, people perceive features categorically—as being either present or not present—and not as a continuum. If a voiced sound—for example, *b*—is produced with some degree of nasalization, listeners perceive either *m* or *b*—they do not perceive some intermediate third sound. In experiments with synthetic speech, for example, subjects will hear either *mad* or *bad*, depending on the amount of nasality that was supplied in synthesizing the initial consonant. Second, only the absolute values + and − are needed for the proper statement of phonological rules. For example, one never has to state that a phonological rule is applicable if *m* has 3 degrees of nasality, *n* has 2 degrees of nasality, *ŋ* has 4 degrees of nasality, and so forth. If the class of nasal phonemes participates in a rule, only the feature [+nasal] (or [−nasal]) is needed to specify that class.

One other point needs to be made before we state rule 1 in its final form. The consonants in part D of rule 1 all share the property of being voiced; that is, they all have the feature [+voiced]. These consonants thus constitute a *natural class* of phonemes that can be defined by a small number of distinctive features. (See *Linguistics*, pp. 110–114, for additional discussion and motivation of the notion "natural class.") Several problems in this workbook (exercises 3.3–3.6) require a phonological rule to be stated in terms of the *distinctive features that define a natural class of phonemes*. Your task in these cases is to find a set of features that will include all of the phonemes in the class and exclude all of the other phonemes in the language. A chart listing the distinctive features of all the phonemes needed for the exercises has been included in appendix 4. (For a description of the features themselves, see *Linguistics*, pp. 103–108.)

To return to rule 2: The phonemes that participate in this rule can be found in appendix 4. It is similar, then, to the intermediate stages you will go through in formulating your rules in exercises 3.3–3.6. In rule 2 the feature that uniquely specifies all of the sounds that undergo vowel lengthening is the feature [+syllabic]. The features that uniquely specify the set of phonemes to the right of the focus bar (part D of the rule) are [+consonantal] and [+voiced]. The feature that specifies part B of the rule is [+long]. (Since there is some question concerning how the feature [+long] is to be represented in phonological theory, it has not been listed as a feature in appendix 4.)

The final form of the rule can now be given as follows:

3. English Vowel-Lengthening Rule (final form)

$$[+\text{syllabic}] \rightarrow [+\text{long}] \ / \ \underline{\qquad} \begin{bmatrix} +\text{consonantal} \\ +\text{voiced} \end{bmatrix}$$

In other words, phonemes that possess the feature [+syllabic] are assigned the feature [+long] whenever they appear before phonemes having the features [+consonantal] and [+voiced].

The answers to exercises 3.3–3.6 require statements similar to rule 3. When only a single phoneme appears in one part of the rule, however, you are usually not required to give its unique distinctive feature specification, although this would be required in a more technical statement of the rule.

3 Transcription Key

Consonants

		Bilabial	Labio-dental	Inter-dental	Dental, Alveolar	Retroflex	Alveo-palatal	Palatal	Velar	Glottal
Stops	voiceless	p			t	ṭ		c	k	ʔ
	voiced	b			d	ḍ		ɟ	g	
Fricatives	voiceless	ɸ	f	θ	s	ṣ	š		x	h
	voiced	β	v	ð	z	ẓ	ž		ɣ	
Affricates	voiceless				tˢ		č			
	voiced				dᶻ		ǰ			
Nasals		m			n	ṇ	ñ		ŋ	
Liquids	lateral				l					
	nonlateral				r	ṛ				
Glides		(w)						y	w(ʍ)	

Additional Symbols
Cʸ = palatalized consonant (for example, tʸ = palatalized t)
C' = glottalized consonant (for example, t' = glottalized (or ejective) t)
' = glottal stop in some transcription systems

Vowels, unrounded

		Front	Central	Back
High	Tense	i(iy)	ɨ	
	Lax	ɪ		
Mid	Tense	e(ey)		
	Lax	ɛ	ʌ(ə)	
Low		æ		ɑ(ay, aw)

Vowels, rounded

		Front	Central	Back
High	Tense	ü		u(uw)
	Lax			ʊ
Mid	Tense	ö		o(ow, oy)
	Lax			ɔ

Additional Symbols
V: = long vowel
Ṽ = nasalized vowel
r̩ = syllabic r. A tick mark under certain resonants (r, l, m, etc.) indicates that the consonant functions as a vowel-like sound.

There are two ways of transcribing the long vowels of English: the IPA system (i, e, o, u) and the Trager-Smith system (iy, ey, ow, uw). Since all four are actually diphthongs (see Linguistics, pp. 76–77), the Trager-Smith system, in which the glides are represented, is the more accurate of the two. Because diphthongs cannot be represented as a single point on a vowel chart, we represent them in terms of the position of their initial vowel.

Sonorant Consonants and Glides: (−syllabic, +sonorant)

	m	n	ṇ	ñ	ŋ	l	r*	ṛ	y	w	h	ʔ
Consonantal	+	+	+	+	+	+	+/−	+	−	−	−	−
Nasal	+	+	+	+	+	−	−	−	−	−	−	−
Lateral	−	−	−	−	−	+	−	−	−	−	−	−
Continuant	−	−	−	−	−	+	+	+	+	+	+	−
Distributed	−	−	−	+	−							
Coronal	−	+	+	+	−	+	+	+	+	−	−	−
Retroflex	−	−	+	−	−	−	−	+	−	−	−	−
Labial	+	−	−	−	−	−	−	−	−	+	−	−
Anterior	+	+	−	−	−	+	+	+	−	−	−	−
High	−	−	−	+	+	−	−	−	+	+	−	−
Back	−	−	−	−	+	−	−	−	−	+	−	−
Strident	−	−	−	−	−	+	−	−	−	−	−	−

Obstruents: (−syllabic, +consonantal, −sonorant)

−Voiced	p	ϕ	f	θ	t	s	tˢ	ṭ	ṣ	š	č	c	k	x
+Voiced	b	β	v	ð	d	z	dᶻ	ḍ	ẓ	ž	ǰ	ɟ	g	ɣ
Nasal	−	−	−	−	−	−	−	−	−	−	−	−	−	−
Lateral	−	−	−	−	−	−	−	−	−	−	−	−	−	−
Continuant	−	+	+	+	−	+	−	−	+	+	−	−	−	+
Distributed				−	−	−	−	−	−	+	+			
Coronal	−	−	−	+	+	+	+	+	+	+	+	−	−	−
Retroflex	−	−	−	−	−	−	−	+	+	−	−	−	−	−
Labial	+	+	+	−	−	−	−	−	−	−	−	−	−	−
Anterior	+	+	+	+	+	+	+	−	−	−	−	−	−	−
High	−	−	−	−	−	−	−	−	−	+	+	+	+	+
Back	−	−	−	−	−	−	−	−	−	−	−	−	+	+
Strident	−	−	+	−	−	+	+	−	+	+	+	−	−	−
Delayed release (affricate)	−	−	−	−	−	−	+	−	−	−	+	−	−	−

*r is [−consonantal] in English but [+consonantal] in other languages.

Vowels: (+syllabic, −consonantal, +sonorant)

	i	ɪ	ɨ	ü	u	ʊ	e	ɛ	ʌ(ə)	o	ö	ɔ*	æ	ɑ
High	+	+	+	+	+	+	−	−	−	−	−	−	−	−
Low	−	−	−	−	−	−	−	−	−	−	−	+/−	+	+
Back**	−	−	+	−	+	+	−	−	+	+	−	+	−	+
Round	−	−	−	+	+	+	−	−	−	+	+	+	−	−
Tense	+	−			+	−	+	−		+	+			

* This symbol represents a low back rounded vowel in English. In other languages it represents a mid lax back rounded vowel.

** The central and back vowels given in the transcription key (appendix 3) all have the feature [+back].

5 Some Phrase Structure Rules for English

For discussion of phrase structure rules, see *Linguistics*, chapter 5.

1. S → NP (Aux) VP
2. NP → (Art) N (PP)
3. NP → (Poss) N
4. Poss → NP Poss-Affix
5. NP → NP Conjunction NP
6. NP → (Q) N (Mod)
7. VP → V $\left(\left\{ \begin{array}{c} NP \\ S \end{array} \right\} \right)$
8. VP → V (NP) (PP)
9. V → V Particle
10. PP → P NP

Mod = Modifier
Art = Article
Poss = Possessive
Q = Quantifier
P = Preposition

6 Grimm's Law

Grimm's Law involves a set of sound changes that took place in Proto-Germanic, in which Proto-Indo-European voiced stops became voiceless stops, voiceless stops became voiceless fricatives, and voiced aspirated stops became simple voiced stops.

Grimm's Law

a. b → p
   d → t
   g → k
b. p → f
   t → θ
   k → x (>h)
c. bh → b
   dh → d
   gh → g

7 The Message Model of Linguistic Communication

The Message Model of linguistic communication may be described as follows:

A speaker has some message in mind that she wants to communicate to a hearer. The speaker then produces some expression from the language that encodes the message as its meaning. Upon hearing the beginning of the expression, the hearer begins identifying the incoming sounds, syntax, and meanings; then, using her knowledge of language, she composes these meanings in the form of a successfully decoded message. (*Linguistics*, p. 346)

According to the Message Model, then, the question "How does successful communication work?" can be answered as follows:

Linguistic communication is successful if the hearer receives the speaker's message. It works because messages have been conventionalized as the meaning of expressions, and by sharing knowledge of the meaning of an expression, the hearer can recognize a speaker's message—the speaker's communicative intention. (*Linguistics*, p. 351)

See pages 348–351 of *Linguistics* for a discussion of problems that arise with the Message Model.

8 Major Moods

Expressions of a language can be used to perform the following *speech acts:*

1. Questioning
2. Stating, promising, threatening, predicting
3. Requesting, commanding, ordering, pleading

Correlated with each type of speech act is a *condition of satisfaction:*

1. Questioning is correlated with an "answerhood condition."
2. Stating is correlated with a "truth condition."
3. Requesting is correlated with a "compliance condition."

Each speech act/satisfaction condition pair is in turn correlated with a *form.* The resulting triple is termed an instance of a particular *mood:*

1. Questioning is associated, directly, with the interrogative mood.
2. Stating is associated with the declarative mood.
3. Requesting is associated with the imperative mood.

The following are examples, in English, of the three major moods.

Interrogative mood

1. Will he leave?

The person who utters sentence 1 is performing a speech act of questioning, which requires the hearer to supply the speaker with the answer. That is, the answerhood condition is operative.

Declarative mood

2. John left the room.

Taken as a statement (i.e., as an instance of the speech act of stating), sentence 2 is either true or false. Truth or falsity is the relevant notion here—the truth condition is operative.

Imperative mood

3. Leave the room!

Taken as an order (i.e., as an instance of the speech act of ordering), sentence 3 involves compliance. The hearer is to do what the sentence describes (in this case, the speaker intends that the hearer leave the room). The compliance condition is operative.

For each language the speech act/satisfaction condition/form pairing is different. That is, different languages choose different syntactic, morphological, and/or phonological (intonation) devices to signal the major moods.

9 Index of Languages

Language	Language family	Principal area where spoken	Exercise
Chinese	Sino-Tibetan	China	5.8, 8.13
Copala Trique	Otomanguean	Mexico	8.12
Dyirbal	Pama-Nyungan	Australia	4.15
Finnish	Finno-Ugric	Finland	8.11
French	Indo-European	Europe	3.8, 3.9
German	Indo-European	Europe	4.11
Greek	Indo-European	Greece	7.2
Japanese	Japanese	Japan	2.7, 3.5, 3.6, 4.16, 4.17, 4.25, 4.26
Korean	Korean	Korea	3.2
Latin	Indo-European		7.2
Nahuatl	Uto-Aztecan	Mexico	4.20
Navajo	Athabascan	North America	5.8, 8.14
Russian	Indo-European	Russia	1.5, 4.24
Spanish	Indo-European	Spain, New World	2.5
Swahili	Niger-Congo	Africa	4.19
Tamil	Dravidian	India	4.12
Telugu	Dravidian	India	4.18
Tohono O'odham	Uto-Aztecan	North America	1.8, 1.9, 3.3, 4.13
Turkish	Ural-Altaic	Turkey	1.7
Yaqui	Uto-Aztecan	North America	4.14
Zoque	Mixe-Zoque	Mexico	3.4